Data Architecture F

The Data Model Toolkit

Simple Skills To Model The Real World

Published by Paragon Publishing

ISBN 978-1-78222-473-0

Book design, layout and production management by Into Print
www.intoprint.net
+44 (0)1604 832149

Printed and bound in UK and USA by Lightning Source

Contents

The Deliverables

Introduction

"The Data Model Is Finished!"

Naturally the startling revelation of this title caught my attention.

Intrigued, I read on.

The article's premise was that with the advent of Big Data we no longer need to waste effort putting together complex and time consuming data models. In this transformed data landscape, everything can be developed rapidly to meet a specific set of requirements. As soon as the next set of requirements arises, if the previous development does not fit them, it will be jettisoned and replaced.

Part of me wondered at this thinking; can the world's organisations now *really* operate in this way because the data landscape been so utterly transformed by Big Data?

I remembered back to similar articles I had read over the years. Each repetition of this death knell has occurred with the advent of a major new paradigm on the data landscape. Examples over the years include; Object-Oriented modelling, Agile development, the relentless advance of COTS[1] products, the Internet and, of course, the Cloud.

But still the data model has survived.

My mind started to sift the evidence that I have personally witnessed. Big Data certainly has had a significant impact on organisations that require data to support their operations, and therefore also on their data models. But I can see no indication that even this seismic shift in data collection and analysis, has caused these core organisational definitions to die out.

In fact, for many organisations, a key outcome of adopting Big Data has been the exact opposite, it has resulted in the realisation of their importance. The explosion of technical innovations that have transformed data usage by organisations, has fundamentally altered the *way* that data models are required to support them in this data-rich environment.

Whereas, in previous times they may have been restricted to being viewed as an 'unwelcome' but necessary part of development, now they are being recognised for what they truly are; a definition of the operational lifeblood of an organisation.

---

1   Commercial off the Shelf

In the last decade data models have made the transition from being ad-hoc and limited in scope, to becoming a central pillar of the Enterprise Architectural landscape.

There is now a realisation that data models allow an organisation to 'know thyself'.

In fact arguably, data models are now more important than ever. It is only with a full and agreed understanding of the 'What?', 'When?' and 'How?' of an organisation's data structures and flows, that we can contemplate plugging COTS products together, implementing in the Cloud and reporting *across* the Enterprise system landscape.

A crucial by-product from the adoption of Big Data is the realisation that its true benefit cannot be delivered without being able to correlate the *meaning* from Big Data analysis with the organisation's Master Data Domains. This has driven the focus for organisations to be able to bring their Master Data under control and thus the processes that manage it.

So, I took what I could from the article, finished my sandwich, and went back to agonising over whether a particularly troublesome Relationship was Transferrable or not.

How To Use This Book

So data models are vitally important, but what exactly are they, how do we create them and, importantly, how do we maximise their benefit?

This book has been written to answer exactly these questions and is constructed with three distinct parts:

The Foundations: What are the solid foundations required for building effective data models?

The Tools: What Tools will enable you to specify clear, precise and accurate data model definitions?

The Deliverables: What processes will you need to successfully define the models, what will these deliver, and how can we make them beneficial to the organisation?

These parts will allow you to use the book in a variety of ways dependent on your immediate needs. So, for example, you may want to start with the Tools part and then for specific points, refer back to the Foundations or Deliverables parts. Alternatively you could simply follow the pages in the way they are sequenced; it's your book, you decide.

The Book's Signposts

Before starting on your journey through this book, here are a few signposts that you need to be able to recognise as described below.

Key Point 1	*The book contains many Key Points to help you and these are formatted like this.*

Activities that the Data Modeller should consider carrying out are highlighted like this.

Who Are You?

This book is intended to be read by anyone who has an interest in maximising the benefit of an organisation's data by creating and sharing the agreed definitions of it.

It has been written to emphasise the relationship of data with the organisation's *operations*, as opposed to its *systems*. Because of this emphasis, you do not need to understand, or even care about, Relational Database Management Systems or Hadoop Clusters, in order to derive full benefit from it. This makes this book an effective resource for those with little or no technical background

However, its emphasis is equally relevant for those with a technical background who, for example, realise they need to stop thinking about data solely in terms of BI reporting.

Of course, these are the ends of a spectrum and you may be positioned somewhere between the two. Wherever you are positioned on it though, what unites you with the other people on it is an interest in maximising the benefit your organisation can make from its data usage.

One of the essential cornerstones to enable this benefit is an operational data model. What we mean by this, is truly a Normalised Logical Data Model.

Irrespective of your personal drivers for reading this book, the journey through its chapters will provide you with a Toolkit that will allow you to successfully create these data models. It also defines processes to enable the data models to accurately reflect the organisation's shared understanding of its data, and to provide the maximum benefit from them.

I sincerely hope that reading this book will bring real benefits to you and to the organisations in which you work.

Dave Knifton

The Logical Data Model defines
the Enterprise data required
by an organisation and
therefore provides it with an
essential foundation
to survive and thrive.

The Foundations

1: Data Models And The Real World

Introduction

I firmly believe that creating and maintaining data models is one of the most important endeavours for all but the smallest organisations!

This is a bold claim, but my argument runs like this; the vast majority of organisations survive and thrive only if their data flows allow them to operate optimally. The success of these flows relies on the shared understanding across the organisation of its data, and it is this understanding that is defined and communicated using data models.

Therefore, for any except the smallest organisations, establishing and sharing this collective understanding through data models should be one of the most important contributors to their ongoing success.

With this in mind, the purpose of this book is to take you on a journey through which you will learn the significance of data models, and the techniques required to create, share and maximise the benefit from them.

Before we start on this journey though, we need to do some preparatory groundwork and it is the job of these first chapters to describe the basic foundations on which our journey will rely.

Data models need to be representations of Real World data, and we cannot possibly start our journey until we establish exactly what we mean by this.

Is The Data Model Finished Yet?

In a world where organisations increasingly snap together Commercial off the Shelf (COTS) products linked though Web Services and hosted in the Cloud, what on earth are we still doing creating data models?

The origin of data models lay, many years ago, in the need to specify data structures required for system development; even today some people still believe that this is the extent of their scope.

Although the world has moved on a great deal since those days and custom development is the exception rather than the norm, data models remain crucially important for organisations in today's world. This is because they provide a detailed specification of the data that flows through any organisation's veins.

They literally define its lifeblood.

Without such data flows, most (certainly all the larger) organisations' operations are brought to a grinding halt *very quickly*. For evidence of this, just think of the enormous sums of money organisations spend on providing and verifying back-up and fail-over capability for so many of the world's systems.

Whether we are; selecting an appropriate COTS product, or hooking bespoke systems together through Web Service calls, or feeding data into Consolidation Hubs or Data Warehouses, we face the same fundamental questions:

- **What** is the **data**?

- **How** is it **defined** and **structured**?

- **When** is it **captured** and **modified**?

- **Where** are its **sources** and **destinations**?

- **Who** has **control** and **access** to which **parts** of it?

Arguably, it is because data models can help us to provide the answers to these questions that they are now more important than ever. Where they used to be isolated within each system development, all organisations are now beginning to appreciate the importance of them at an Enterprise level.

What Are Data Models?

We have described that the definitions of appropriate data flows are crucial to healthy organisations, but where exactly does the data model fit into establishing their definition? In order to fully understand what data models deliver, we need to firstly understand what *data* is, and its relationship with organisations.

At its very simplest, we can think of data as providing a description of the Real World in a way that allows us to collectively make sense of it.

Key Point 2   *Data reveals the <u>truth</u> about what is going on in the Real World.*

Within this definition of data, are *transactions* that record events and their outcomes. These events are meaningless in themselves. It is only when we create *definition frameworks* that establish their *meaning* and provide context for them that they become understood and therefore can yield benefit.

Figure 1 – Data without meaning

In the example in figure 1, the value **750** has magnitude but still *means* nothing to us.

Figure 2 – Data with meaning

In figure 2 we see that adding a meaning framework around the value, results in it being placed into a context that allows us to fully understand its significance.

> **Key Point 3**   *Data can only have meaning for us when we construct a <u>meaning framework</u> around it.*

Meaning in data

The exchange of data's *meaning* provides the basis for all interactions and operations; both internally throughout an organisation, and externally into the environment in which it operates. Yet many times in discussions about data definitions, it seems as if the meaning of data is somehow an optional extra. How many times do we hear variations of this snippet?

'Oh don't worry about what it's called; I'll put something in for that later ...'

Unfortunately for Data Modellers, this 'meaning as optional extra' approach is unacceptable, since these *meanings* constitute the very heart of an organisation's interactions with its data. Therefore they must form the basis of the definitions of their data models.

> **Key Point 4**   *To maximise the benefit of the definitions and flows of data across an organisation, they need to have an Enterprise-wide view.*

The consequences of Key Point 4 are explained in the following section.

Enterprise Data

The meaning of data is almost everything, but in fact there is a nuance we need to add to it.

> **Key Point 5**   *For organisations, the universally understood and agreed meaning of data is everything.*

Therefore to optimise data's benefit throughout an organisation, there must be consistent *meaning* applied to it *across* the organisation. If this is achieved we consider the data definitions to be of Enterprise significance.

> ***Key Point 6***   ***We can consider the data to be Enterprise Data if a uniformity of meaning of it can be established <u>across</u> the organisation.***

There is another more subtle and often ignored aspect to this shared *meaning,* and this is to do with the stakeholders involved in the use of an organisation's data. To maximise the data's benefit to an organisation, these stakeholders must *share* the organisation's *universally agreed definitions* of the data.

In other words, what people in one part of an organisation think a 'Primary Outlet Location' means should be exactly the same as what someone from a totally different area thinks it means[2].

> ***Key Point 7***   ***The meaning of data can truly only be of Enterprise significance, if all of the organisation's stakeholders <u>share</u> the same Enterprise definitions of the data.***

So how can this shared meaning be effectively communicated across the organisation to all the relevant stakeholders?

We will discuss the impact of this challenge on the data modelling processes later in the book.

So far though, we have not considered the events that initially create the data, and subsequently modify it through its Lifecycle.

We have already mentioned that data records the changes associated with events that occur within the organisation's view of the Real World, for example, 'Receipt of a Payment'. These events are themselves largely driven, and responded to, by *activities*.

It is therefore critical to understand the activities within an organisation that cause and, in turn, are caused by these events. This is because they define

---

2   With the caveat that they may use synonymous terms.

the way that an organisation *interacts* with its data. Understanding this, will allow us to define the data states and outcomes and therefore create their surrounding framework of meaning.

Key Point 8   *Only by understanding the activities required by an organisation can we fully understand how data underpins its operations.*

Therefore, to fully and accurately define an organisation's data usage, it is crucial to understand its activities, and so we need to define a way to think about them.

Process Versus Function

Data models do not come from nowhere.

They must represent definitions and structures of data that allow the organisation to operate optimally. Because of this, they must be based on what an organisation *does*, or maybe more importantly, what it *should be doing*.

But from where will Data Modellers gain this understanding?

The understanding can only come from definitions of activities that constitute the organisation's operations.

As a consequence, Data Modellers cannot be divorced from these activities and in fact, it is critically important for them to have a thorough understanding of these core operational activities.

Key Point 9   *A comprehensive understanding of an organisation's relationship with its data, can only be derived from definitions of the activities that determine its usage.*

For data models to allow an organisation to thrive, they must be insulated from poorly implemented or redundant activities, and instead be based upon *ideal* definitions of these activities.

Processes and Functions provide one way of differentiating what organisations are *actually* doing, from what they *should* be doing. This idea will allow us to develop a simple thought framework with which we can radically improve the benefit of our data models to the organisation.

For the basis of this framework, I will lean heavily on Richard Barker's definitions[3]. This is because over the years, I have found his clear way of thinking has proved extremely useful.

Processes

Processes describe what activities are *actually* carried out by an organisation.

> *Key Point 10*   *Processes specify __what__ activities an organisation __actually__ carries out.*

Since Process definitions are specified within the context of the way that the organisation carries out activities today, today's *mechanisms* typically become embedded into their definitions. What we mean by this term 'mechanism', is the physical way that an activity is carried out, for example, '**Type and send an email** confirming the Order details to the Client'.

> *Key Point 11*   *Process definitions are prone to incorporating the __mechanisms__ that specify the way activities are carried out __today__.*

Functions

In contrast to Processes, Functions are *abstracted* definitions of the activities that an organisation *should* carry out, in order to be successful now *and into the future*.

---

3   From Richard Barker's CASE*Method Function and Process Modelling book. ISBN-13: 978-0201565256.

> **Key Point 12** *Functions are <u>abstracted</u> definitions of activities that an organisation <u>needs</u> to perform, in order to survive and <u>thrive into the future</u>.*

Because these activity definitions are abstracted, they must not make references to any specific mechanism that could be used to carry them out.

So instead of 'Type and send an email confirming the Order details to the Client', an equivalent Function would specify 'Communicate the Order confirmation details to the Client'.

> **Key Point 13** *Function definitions are abstracted and therefore should not include any mechanisms used to perform them.*

In fact, we can think of these as *'idealised* Processes', that is, they describe purely *what* activities need to be carried out, but are totally agnostic to the way that they are actually executed.

Successful Organisations

Figure 3 illustrates schematically the difference between Processes and Functions in terms of the activities that an organisation carries out.

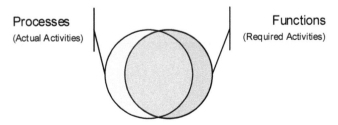

Figure 3 - Functions versus Processes

Highly successful organisations make sure that what they *are* doing is exactly what they *should* be doing. Obviously the lower the degree of overlap, the more opportunity there is for an organisation to re-engineer its Processes and improve its operational effectiveness.

Although Data Modellers need not be concerned with Process versus Function per se, as a core principle they should ensure that their models are future-proofed against any changes caused by the re-engineering of underpinning Processes.

This is because in a bid to re-engineer an organisation's Processes to be more efficient, mechanisms may need to be replaced. If data models are resilient to mechanistic changes, then any changes to systems or activities that use them as a foundation, should not require them to be re-defined.

In other words, we shouldn't need to revisit our data models simply because an automated Process replaces a manual one.

> ***Key Point 14*** ***To make data models more resilient to any changes in operational Processes, they should be based upon <u>abstracted</u> Function definitions, rather than <u>mechanistic</u> Process definitions.***

Of course, removing mechanisms is not always possible, and some mechanistic definitions may be *required*. Often this is as a result of legislative or regulatory requirements. For example, within regulated markets notifications are often required from participants, and the mechanisms for these notifications, such as an email address, are typically prescribed.

However, as Data Modellers, we also need to factor into our models the reality that regulations and legislation and even their adjudication bodies will *inevitably* change over time and will certainly differ across the globe.

Models versus Reality

At this point we need to remind ourselves what it is that we are trying to achieve; we are learning how to construct *models* of *data*.

It therefore makes sense that we should derive our understanding of the meaning of the activities, from well-defined and agreed *models* of these *activities*.

This is because such models will already have simplified, standardised and abstracted the activities that operational people believe are required. This will provide an immeasurably improved source for activity definitions compared with the original ad-hoc, incomplete and possibly anecdotal evidence.

Hopefully these models will also be much closer to Function definitions than

Process definitions, although some critical review should be applied to verify that this is the case.

Figure 4 shows how the data and related activity models have Real World reflections.

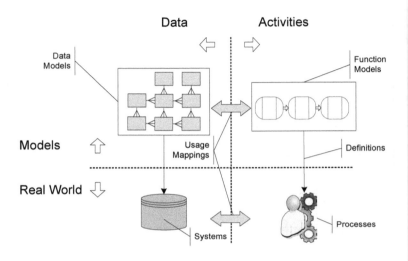

Figure 4 - Models versus the Real World

Standard Operating Models

Many organisations attempt to standardise the way that they carry out their operations. This can produce major benefits for the organisation, including easier on-boarding of new staff and providing consistency in the delivery of their products and services.

The way that they do this is by defining a Standard Operating Model[4] (SOM) which aims to define a standardised blueprint of the way that an organisation should carry out its activities. A well-defined SOM should also specify the way that data is used within the activity definitions at a low level of detail.

Any SOM models need to be a part of the discovery Artifacts for Data Modellers, since they can be a well-defined catalogue of the activities that require, create and maintain data.

---

4   Sometimes this concept is interchangeably referred to as Standard Operating Procedures (SOP).

> **Key Point 15**   *SOM definitions should be used as a key resource for Data Modellers, since they define the interactions an organisation's operations have with its data.*

SOM models can be invaluable when defining the scope, structure and detail of the data required by an organisation.

However, a degree of caution should be exercised in assuming that these models accurately represent what is *really* carried out within the organisation, as:

- the initial analysis may be flawed

- the organisation may have 'moved on' since the definitions were captured

- people are remarkably adept at ignoring the way that they are told to do something!

Additionally, the extent of the SOM definitions must not be assumed to accurately define the scope boundaries of the data models[5].

The Data Modeller needs to exercise caution when using SOM definitions as the basis for their data models. This is because they typically contain a lot of mechanistic references. Of course any such references need to be abstracted when specifying any data elements gleaned from the models.

Organisation Awareness

Now we have looked at Processes and Functions as a way of conceptualising an organisation's operational activities, let's consider the stakeholders within the organisation. An organisation has a relationship with its data that is established through its stakeholders and therefore we must consider how they can contribute to the definition of our data models.

Typically, everyone who works for an organisation is aware of their relationship with it and are also familiar with at least some of the other stakeholders of the organisation.

---

5   There is more detail of how to define the data model scope in chapter 18.

Awareness model of an organisation's activities

In the head of every stakeholder of an organisation is a complex set of knowledge, behaviours, expectations and value judgements about; the organisation, the way that it operates and, in particular, the way that it relates to that stakeholder.

This set of complex personal attributes can be thought of as an Awareness Set.

Imagine the Awareness Set representation for an individual employee as illustrated in Figure 5.

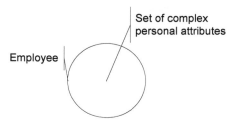

Figure 5 - Individual Awareness Set model

This employee works alongside a colleague on a day to day basis and therefore their individual Awareness Sets have a large degree of overlap. We can represent this as a second Awareness Set overlapping that of the first employee.

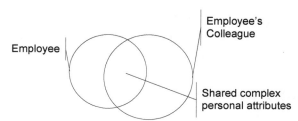

Figure 6 - Shared Awareness Set model

The two individuals report to a line manager who knows something about what they do and how they do it, but does not know all of the detail. The manager, however, does have knowledge about the way the organisation operates in other areas.

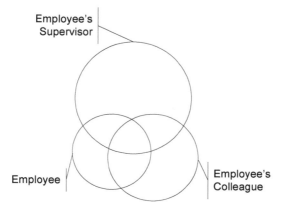

Figure 7 - Supervisor shared Awareness Set model

We can keep on adding more and more Awareness Sets to this picture for the organisation. But, as we extend the model, a two and even three dimensional representation becomes increasingly difficult. This is because the Awareness Sets have extremely complex overlaps in all but the simplest organisations.

Importantly though, notice that; although *how* the organisation operates is dependent on the combined set, it is extremely rare for any, other than the smallest organisations, to have a single stakeholder who has an overall understanding about:

- *all* of the operations carried out by an organisation

- the characteristics of *all* of its stakeholders and

- *their* interactions with the organisation

In fact, this is a significant problem for the Data Modeller because ideally they need to operate with an understanding and knowledge based upon the 'big picture' for the organisation.

The Subject Matter Expert

An individual SME's Awareness Set, has the special characteristic that it contains a significant intersection with many of the Awareness Sets for individuals who operate in specific areas.

We can think of the SME's Awareness Set profile looking like the schematic in figure 8.

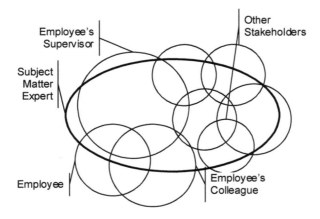

Figure 8 - Subject Matter Expert Awareness Set model

To mitigate the problem of not having a <u>single</u> stakeholder that has the 'big picture' for an organisation, the Data Modeller must seek out and communicate effectively with Subject Matter Experts (SMEs).
Therefore as a key enabler to working in any particular operational areas, the Data Modeller needs to establish a list of SMEs and create an effective working relationship with them.

Engaging with SMEs

Often though, engaging with SMEs can be much harder than it sounds!

Not only can finding the correct SMEs be difficult, but often these are the very individuals who have the least time to spare. This is usually because their expertise is in extremely high demand.

We will look in more detail at the way the Data Modeller needs to engage with key stakeholders including SMEs in chapter 17.

2: The Data Model As A Communication Tool

Introduction

For many organisations, whether they realise it or not, data models can provide one of the most powerful tools they have at their disposal to improve their operations and strategies.

Data models can achieve this by specifying, communicating and facilitating agreement on a common set of definitions of the data's meaning and patterns that can be used throughout the organisation.

It is this communication purpose that makes data models so important.

On our brief journey so far, we have learned about the importance of a shared meaning framework for our data definitions. We will now learn how data models facilitate this communication across the organisation.

This chapter describes the factors that influence the success of this communication and describes some simple techniques that can be used to gain *more* benefit from the process of data modelling.

In addition to improving the benefit derived from your data models, these techniques have the added bonus of reducing the amount of effort required to define them!

The Data Model As A Communication Tool

It cannot be over-emphasised that the *only* reason that data models exist is to *communicate* understanding and facilitate *agreement* on, data's *meanings* and *patterns* that are relevant to an organisation.

> *Key Point 16*   *The only reason for creating and maintaining data models is so that they can be used as a communication tool to <u>share</u> the <u>agreed understanding</u> of its data <u>across an organisation</u>.*

Once we understand that this is their true purpose, we realise that it is essential that their *key* characteristic is *clarity*. They must convey the meaning of the data easily and unequivocally to all of the organisation's stakeholders.

With this in mind, let's think about the features that enable the data model to be an effective communication tool.

The impact of data model syntax

We must always remember that data models use symbols and that these will convey different meanings to different people, including potentially *nothing at all!*

Therefore, the understanding provided by a data model will be dependent on its audience to a great degree.

This can be represented in the simple communication model illustrated in figure 9.

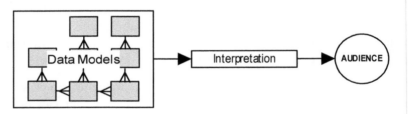

Figure 9 - Data Model interpretation

One of the key factors influencing the successful communication of a data model is the symbolic language used, which can itself change *what* is communicated.

This symbolic language has two important aspects of interpretation that can act:

1. as a communication barrier

2. to skew understanding

These aspects are described in more detail below.

Syntax interpretation barrier

We often believe that data models *facilitate* communication of data patterns and definitions. What can sometimes be forgotten is that data models use a symbolic representation and that not every stakeholder will read them in the same way that you do!

If the data model syntax is not understood by the audience, then it will act as a barrier to, rather than an enabler of, communication.

Consider the example in figure 10.

Figure 10 - You see what I mean?

Unless we understand the symbols, the message is lost!

Key Point 17 *The symbolic representation used in data models can form a barrier to, rather than an enabler of, its understanding.*

This idea was recently brought home to me again when I worked for a client where only a single Business Analyst could possibly read the Enterprise Data Models I had developed. Although this person could read the basic symbols, they still required help in *understanding* some of the more complex areas of the model. All the other stakeholders had only Business and Operational expertise and background. Putting a Logical Data Model in front of them would have proved a disaster!

In order to avoid this negative outcome, I arranged a series of sessions to walk the other stakeholders through the areas of the model using worked examples of the data patterns and meaning. This proved an extremely productive way of conveying the meaning contained in the data model and allowed the stakeholders to fully participate in the data model's definition.

To minimise the impact of the symbolic interpretation creating a communication barrier, the Data Modeller should consider using active processes to guide stakeholders through the meaning defined in the data models.
Of course, even active sessions may not be effective in overcoming the barrier to understanding that a data model's visual symbols present for many stakeholders. The Data Modeller will therefore have to consider using a variety of ways to communicate the <u>meaning</u> of the organisation's data, and these may well not use any symbolic elements at all[6].

---

6   For more detail on the definition and use of a Data Lexicon in this regard, please refer to chapter 17.

Syntax interpretation skews

There is more than one symbolic syntax in general use for data modelling. For example, you are likely to come across all of the following at some point in your data modelling endeavours:

- UML

- Information Engineering

- IDEF1X

- Barker Notation[7]

Bear in mind that adopting these different data modelling syntax definitions can itself skew understanding.

Another often ignored aspect of this is that because tools support different syntax frameworks, the adoption of a particular data modelling *tool* can itself cause the same skewing of understanding.

Key Point 18   *Different data modelling tools can cause a skewing of understanding because of the different syntax frameworks they support.*

Not long ago I came across this very point when working at a client site. The client's tool of choice was an Enterprise tool that is widely used across the globe. This tool though, does not support Barker Notation and so where the model definition required the use of Arcs, I could not represent these on the model.

As a result, I was forced into different representations in the Logical Data Model. This in turn affected the way that the data's understanding was communicated, and could also skew any transitions to Physical Data Models.

Abstraction Barrier

Another significant communication barrier to consider is that the data models are produced using abstraction abilities that not everyone will possess.

Often in these situations the use of concrete examples will pay massive

---

7   Barker Notation is used throughout the Models in this book because it is easy to understand and has simple visual syntax that allows advanced concepts to be modelled elegantly.

dividends. In fact, I would strongly argue that examples are *always* essential in definitions, as I have found they lead to more clarity and reduced ambiguity for *all* stakeholders.

Let's concentrate on some simple techniques that can be used to remove these abstraction barriers.

Abstracting patterns in data modelling

The technique of abstraction is essential in order to uncover patterns from the instances of data. The ability to filter out the 'noise' and specificity of data occurrences, reveals patterns of meaning that are required as the basis for our data models definitions.

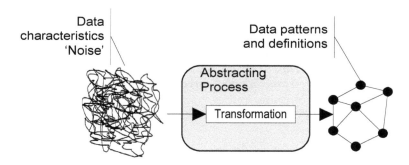

Figure 11 - Abstraction in data modelling

Figure 11 illustrates the role that abstraction plays in defining the data patterns from the somewhat unstructured 'noise' of the data's Real World characteristics.

Key Point 19   *The process of abstraction strips away any specific or mechanistic interpretations and reveals the essence of the data's meaning.*

Abstracting names

Although the Data Modeller needs to avoid mechanistic or other specificity in names, to do this is not as simple as it sounds. Abstracting names away from those terms commonly used in operational areas, can make it difficult for stakeholders to make sense of the data model's definitions.

To help mitigate the problem of creating a communication barrier through the abstraction of names and terms, the Data Modeller should always try to supplement the definitions with synonyms and relevant concrete examples.

Generic structures

Generic structures offer all sorts of advantages particularly by allowing models to be flexible and future-proofed.

The problem with generic structures though, is that they rely upon a degree of abstraction that many in the organisation may not be used to, and as a result can be very difficult to communicate.

The Data Modeller needs to think carefully about whether it is even possible to review generic structures with <u>any</u> stakeholders.
Instead of reviewing the data models directly, they should try to use realistic worked examples of data that the logical structures would hold. Using this approach can clarify the capability offered by such structures to stakeholders, and thus gain their understanding and agreement.

Splattergrams

I use the term Splattergram to describe data models that have been created ignoring their communication purpose and whose layout fails to provide clarity.

Figure 12 is an example of a real Splattergram, a variation of which we have all seen at one time or another.

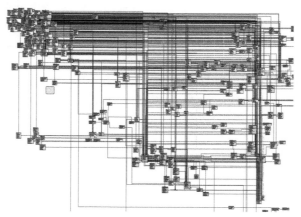

Figure 12 – A real Splattergram

The Data Modeller should ensure that all data models are fit for purpose. At the very least, they must ensure that the data models contain no crossing lines and have no overlapping!

We will return to refining the visual layout of our data models further, a little later on in our journey.

Data model legends

When stakeholders view data models in the absence of any context, it is often very difficult for them to gauge exactly what they are looking at. Therefore always ensure that each model provides its context within the data landscape. Such context can easily be provided by the addition of a simple legend that contains a few headline details.

These should contain at a minimum a:

- Title

- Project or Programme reference

- Revision number

- Date of last revision

- Author/s

Product Definition Subject Area

Programme: Global Data Model
Version: 1.04
Date: 15 August 2018
Author: D Knifton

Figure 13 – An example data model legend

Ensure that the legend is within the boundary of the printable region so that if it is shared, the legend will appear on the shared copies. However, don't forget that it should be placed so that it does not obstruct, or add confusion to the reading of the data model structures.

Data Model Dissemination

There is another aspect to the communication purpose of data models that needs to be considered.

You will spend a lot of effort and the organisation will spend a lot of money creating data model definitions. But will the outcome of this commitment be that the data models languish in a rarefied repository somewhere and only a handful of people in the organisation will occasionally make reference to them? In the future, will people stumble across them only to wonder how current they are, or whether they were ever reflected anywhere in the data landscape of the organisation?

My opinion is that this is not the right destiny for your deliverables and we shall return to this topic to consider alternatives later in the Deliverables part of the book.

3: The Data Modelling Process Overview

Introduction

We now understand the principles and concepts that are required to create a firm basis for our data modelling. We also appreciate the data model's crucial communication purpose, and some basic techniques that can be used to make them achieve this goal more successfully.

This means that we are ready for the next stage on our journey, which is to consider the processes required to create and maintain the data model.

This chapter provides an overview of how the data modelling activities are used to take the characteristics of Real World data, and define a beneficial framework of data structures and meaning from them.

It emphasises that data modelling should fundamentally be an *active* process.

It should not merely consist of a series of deliverable milestones, but must be formed from effective processes carried out by the Data Modeller.

In addition, it is important to remember that it cannot be a solitary endeavour, but it *must* involve a group of key stakeholders. The critical reason for this is that the various viewpoints of different stakeholders will ensure the *accuracy* of the *shared understanding* of the data's meaning.

The Data Modelling Process

Figure 14 illustrates the way that the overall data modelling process consumes the characteristics of an organisation's (rather messy) Real World data and defines a neat, well organised and agreed output from it.

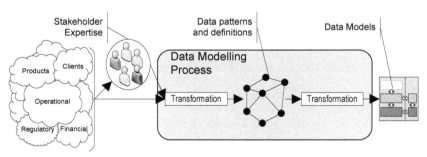

Figure 14 – A Data Modelling Process overview

Importantly, this definition needs to be relevant *to*, and aligned *with*, the organisation for which it is developed. This can be achieved with the commitment and involvement of a number of key stakeholders in the organisation. These stakeholders can also facilitate the easier assimilation of the definitions into the organisation's self-awareness.

Although the schematic in figure 14 helps us to understand how the data's meaning gets extracted and refined into rational definitions, it doesn't illustrate the specific data modelling processes required.

We can transform the Data Modelling Process in figure 14 to a definition of the high level processes as depicted in figure 15.

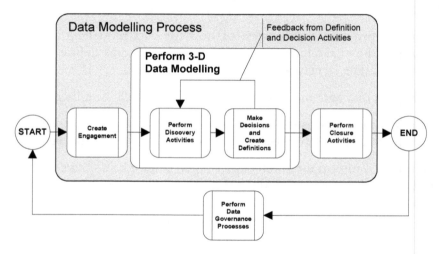

Figure 15 - High Level Data Modelling Processes

The high level processes required are:

- Create Engagement
- Perform 3-D Data Modelling
  - Perform Discovery Activities
  - Make Decisions and Create Definitions
- Perform Closure Activities

These processes are briefly described in the following sections, but are more fully defined in their own dedicated chapters in the Deliverables part of the book.

Create Engagement

I would argue that it is *absolutely essential* for you to have a set of activities at the start of your modelling endeavours to define the specifics of the engagement. These specifics will create the required infrastructure and framework for the successful definition of your data models.

It is during the Engagement Process that you should think through the entire set of activities and consider the organisational framework within which the data modelling activities need to be integrated.

In my experience, however informal you make this process, you will reap big rewards by carrying it out. As the minimum possible outcomes from it, you will need to create commitment from stakeholders and agree exactly what it is that you will be delivering.

It may be that the Engagement Process does not require a great deal of formalisation. But even if you decide that all you need to do is to review the check list in the Data Modelling Approach Template[8], then it will almost certainly yield benefit, since it will focus your mind on the work ahead.

At the very least you must discover and record a list of key stakeholders and think about your communication plan with these individuals. It is the aim of this chapter to describe the broader set of activities that you may well also need to undertake.

Data Modelling In 3-D

The entire data modelling activity is often thought of as a Data Modeller sitting in isolation at a desk, using a tool to churn out data models that they carefully save into a data model repository.

This is fine as an image, but as an approach is highly unlikely to produce any worthwhile results.

Data modelling demands a more *active* focus that should ideally encompass the 'Three Ds', which are to:

- Discover

- Decide

- Define

Their inter-relationships are illustrated in figure 16.

---

8   In appendix A

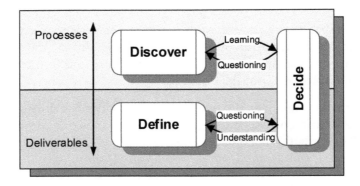

Figure 16 – The 3-D Data Modelling activities

In order to be successful, the 3-D activities cannot be carried out sequentially, or independently. They must be tightly interwoven sets of activities that together constitute the data modelling process.

So what does each of these sets of activities comprise?

The Discover Process

The Discover activities are those that uncover, collate and organise the information from which the data's meaning can be revealed and refined.

These activities are the detective work that Data Modellers need to undertake.

> *Key Point 20*   *The Discover process unearths the raw information that feeds into the data modelling activities.*

Part of what can be Discovered, will be in the form of existing Artifacts. Data Modellers will therefore need to be able to absorb, challenge and distil understanding from these. However, if this sounds easy, in my experience the Artifacts can often present a challenge. This is because they typically contain incomplete and contradictory testimony.

It must always be remembered that even though Artifacts provide some of what needs to be discovered, it is the *active* part of the Discover Process that yields the greatest contribution of information.

Whatever raw information is unearthed by the Discover process will need to be evaluated by the next process which is the Decide process.

The Decide Process

Once elements are discovered, there must be activities that evaluate exactly *what is it* that has actually been discovered.

This evaluation is all about interpretation and cross-referencing the discovery information, and therefore entails decision making. In fact, a constant stream of decisions needs to be made about the structures and definitions that are being created and modified in the data models. Even for very simple models, there are typically a number of different ways of representing very similar meanings of the data.

Naturally, the decisions will be influenced by all sorts of constraints and factors, including your own personality and experience! However, by striving for consensus with a range of stakeholders, any individual idiosyncrasies should be counterbalanced. This will allow the model definitions to provide *accurate* representations that are *appropriate* for the organisation.

Some of the outcomes from the Decide process will be to question the discovery information which can in turn give rise to further discovery activities. Other outcomes from the decisions that you make, will lead to the definitions that you record into your data model.

Key Point 21   *The Decision process is based upon a constant stream of questioning, evaluation and refining outcomes.*

The outputs from the Decide process will be used as the basis for the Define process deliverables.

The Define Process

The Define activities record the outputs from the understanding gained from the Discover and Decide activities.

The activities of this process are the ones that we typically think of as 'data modelling'. It is this set of activities where Data Modellers may legitimately be seen working by themselves, recording the understanding they have refined, into a symbolic and structured representation.

The outputs from the Define activities are the data models themselves and any additional Artifacts such as a Data Lexicon as mentioned earlier in chapter 2.

Key Point 22   *The Define process creates the data models and possibly other related Artifact definitions.*

It is worth emphasising that this activity is simply the *scribing* part of the data modelling process. The formal writing up of your notes, if you will. If the understanding of the data patterns and meaning are flawed, then the data models that are produced from these activities will be flawed as well.

As a consequence therefore, never forget that this recording process must not be unquestioning, and as a result, may well give rise to a further cycle of decision and even discovery activities.

Perform Closure Activities

At the end of the 3-D Data Modelling process, there needs to be a set of Closure activities that are carried out. These activities will be focussed on ensuring the data models provide benefit for the organisation and, as a consequence, are all about their consumers.

Therefore, the effective communication and integration of the data modelling deliverables throughout the organisation, must be a key part of the Closure process.

Key Point 23   *The Closure process is all about the <u>dissemination</u> and <u>integration</u> of the data model definitions throughout the data landscape of your organisation, in order to provide maximum benefit from them.*

A growing number of organisations have created Data Governance Frameworks to gain control of their data definitions. Ideally any Data Governance Framework should see data models as cornerstones of their robust definition and hopefully you will be working within such an organisation.

If this is the case, then processes should already be defined that will respond to the changes in the data definitions that are formalised in your data models. These processes will therefore prescribe the way that the data model's definitions need to be communicated to all relevant stakeholders.

However, your organisation may not have a mature Data Governance Framework, or even if it has, it may not see the data models as providing the crucial bed-rock of its foundation.

If you face either of these scenarios, there may not be any recognition of the importance of communicating the outcomes from the data modelling processes. As a result, you will need to agree with key stakeholders the way the data model definitions *will* be assimilated into the organisation's data landscape. In other words, how will the outputs from the data modelling process be consumed across the organisation *and* bring real benefit to it?

Data Model Longevity

Just before we start to define the Tools for our Toolkit, here is a strange and maybe surprising thing to consider; think of some organisations and play back their data domains 20, 50 or even 100 years.

For many organisations, the fundamental Real World data relating to their operational inputs, processes or outcomes has not changed significantly over these timeframes!

Key Point 24   *Accurate data models, within an organisation's data scope, will remain true representations over extended periods of time.* [9]

As an example, imagine a car manufacturer; their contemporary data model should be fairly consistent with one that could (hypothetically) have been created a hundred years ago!

This is especially true for manufacturing industries, but possibly less obvious,

---

9   The caveats for this Key Point are that the model was originally not mechanistic and was *accurate*. For more detail on how we determine the accuracy of models please refer to chapter 18.

is that it is also relevant for other more data-centric industries, such as insurance.

What this implies is that it is worth the time and effort to get data models 'correct', since the transformational benefits can be long lasting.

If data models do require updating significantly within a few years, then this may well be an indication that they weren't that well thought through originally.

A common cause of the reduced longevity of models is that they contain mechanistic definitions.

In recent times another significant cause of changes has been the advent of the Internet. As an example, location based operations which used to only correspond to physical locations, could now be associated with more virtual locations, as exemplified by on-line purchasing.

Of course more recently we have also witnessed the dramatic impact and rapid ascendancy of Big Data. As a result of the explosion of data creation and capture, there has been a direct impact on data models and their scope has been expanded.

A lot of the increased scope is the ability to record aspects of the external environment in which the organisation operates, for example, 'consumer sentiment'.

Thus data models need to be extended in order to incorporate key elements from these new data realms. Our data models now need to provide the context with which these new data sets can be referenced with our operational data.

The internals of our organisation's operations may have changed very little despite this revolution. But at the boundaries of the organisation's internal world and the external world in which it operates, we need to carefully assess how we are able to link these two worlds through our data structures. We will examine these pivotal changes to our data models in chapter 15.

The Tools

4: The Names Of Things
– Entities

Introduction

On our journey so far, we have established that data models are essential for an organisation in order to define, agree and share the understanding of its data's meaning. We have also gained an overview of the processes that are required to successfully develop our data models.

With these solid foundations established, we are ready to start to define the Tools that are needed to construct our data models.

The type of data models these Tools will allow us to construct are often called Logical Data Models. They area also commonly known as Entity Relationship Data Models, or simply Normalised Data Models.

Logical Data Models are created using visual elements to define the data's meaning, structures and patterns.

In this chapter we will start to learn how to specify the most basic visual building blocks for these. We'll start at the very beginning which is to learn how to define the data elements we call Entities.

In a nutshell, Entities are the *things* of *significance* about which an organisation needs to capture data in order to support and understand its operations. In terms of our Toolkit, Entities form the basic data elements of our data model definitions.

Entities

Entities are often described as the occurrences of 'significant things', about which the organisation must capture data, in order to survive and thrive. They are the basic building blocks of data used to record and provide context for an organisation's activities.

> **Key Point 25**   *Entities are the definitions of 'things' that have significance within the scope of the Organisation's operations, about which data <u>needs</u> to be captured.* [10]

Many Entities are quite concrete; we could touch them or sense them directly in some way. Others are far more abstract and therefore may not be immediately obvious to anyone within the organisation.

Entity syntax

Let's start by looking at a very simple example.

Since you are reading this book, I can definitely rely on it as an example that is within your experience.

Figure 17 – A simple Entity

Notice that it has some visual syntax features.

Entities are represented as soft cornered boxes and each must have a name in the singular that describes *what* the 'thing' *is*, that we are defining.

The Organisation Entity

So now we have seen the simple visual syntax of Entities, let's look at a Real World example.

Most organisations in the world are interested in maintaining some degree of understanding about other organisations. Typically, this is because these other organisations provide products or services to it, or consume products or services from it.

---

10   Entities can still have validity within an Organisation's scope even if it is not possible to currently source their data. For discussion of this, see the Known and Knowable section in chapter 17.

I am absolutely confident you will encounter this Entity more than once in your data modelling activities. This makes it an obvious choice to use as an example, to help us understand how to data model.

Figure 18 - Simple Organisation Entity

As we acquire more Tools on our journey, we will use them to refine this basic definition of the Organisation Entity.

Discovering Entities

When teaching Entity Relationship data modelling, the simple technique of recording the *nouns* found in communications and documentation, is often used to describe how to start data modelling. These nouns will certainly help you to produce an initial list of Entities, since they describe the 'things' about which the organisation is interested.

Although this is not the sole technique available, using it will definitely kick-start the process of recording and defining the significant Entities within your organisation's scope.

The definition of an Organisation would seem to be very simple and unambiguous, but the more time you spend trying to figure out what is meant by an Organisation, the more blurred the definition can become.

At first glance its definition would appear to be self-evident, for example, 'A Company that we do business with'. But even this definition starts to reveal the layers of meaning that you could be tempted to peel back[11]. For example, what do we mean by a Company?

There are many different types of Organisations that are not Companies in the strict legal sense, for example, Charities and Healthcare Trusts. We will explore these issues and how to resolve them as we add more sophistication to our Tools later. At this stage let's discover how to add more rigour to our Entity definitions.

11   This is a good example of the constant stream of decisions required by data modelling that was described earlier within the Decide Process.

Defining Entities

This section concentrates on describing the characteristics that need to be fully specified to define our Entities.

Entity names

Years ago I learned the basics of data modelling from Richard Barker[12], who insisted that the Entity names should be singular and in uppercase. These days I am not so hung up on their names being in uppercase, but I still believe that the Entity is an occurrence of *a* thing of significance, and therefore should be named in the singular.

So for example:

- Person

- Organisation

- Order

- Payment

When creating the names of your Entities, watch out for common undetected contraventions of this singular naming convention, for example:

- Event **Log** ⇨ Event

- Order **History** ⇨ Order

- Product **List** ⇨ Product

One of the other things that I learned from Richard Barker is that the name is of *paramount importance*.

Key Point 26   ***The name of an Entity is of the utmost importance for defining and sharing its meaning.***

My understanding of the importance of this core principle has only got stronger over the years. In fact, making careful decisions about your choice for the names needs to be a key part of getting your models 'correct'.

---

12   One of the founders of Oracle UK.

For example, at first sight the following Entity names would appear to be interchangeable:

- Person

- Contact

- Employee

But actually, they do not represent the same *thing* at all!

Each has a slightly different connotation, and these subtle differences will influence the way that each is thought of in the context of the organisation's operations. This means that decisions must always be made as to which name *most accurately* reflects the Entity's meaning in your model.

Where the other names are synonymous, you must make decisions as to whether it is worthwhile to record them as Synonyms of the Entity.

You should record them if:

1. they are used within the organisation to mean the same thing

2. the terms are *not* used within the organisation, but you think they may allow those who are unfamiliar with it, to understand the Entity

3. you have abstracted an Entity based on one or more concrete Entities, and need to use these names with stakeholders so that they can still recognise it

If the names are not synonymous, then you must decide whether they are really different 'things' and therefore need to be recorded as new Entities in your data model.

But notice that there is a potential conflict in the naming of our Entities.

Earlier we saw that the agreed meaning of data is critical and that all stakeholders need to have input and review the definitions of the Entities. However, we have also learned in chapter 1 that is important to abstract away from the *now* and ignore any mechanistic interpretations.

This means that we may need to choose names that are not immediately recognisable by key stakeholders in the organisation.

The decision making process for the Entity name is often not all that easy. Of course, as you come to understand the data more thoroughly, the initial choice of a name may need to be replaced because your understanding has become clearer.

Entity description

Once you have identified and recorded an Entity's name, the next thing to define is its description.

The description needs to be concise and provide an easy to read understanding of what the Entity represents. It needs to be worded in plain language that key stakeholders can understand and agree to.

To help solidify the definition in the readers' minds it is a good idea to include at least one example, of course, two or three is always better.

> **Key Point 27** *Recording examples in the Entity definition always helps by bringing the Entity 'to life' and removes ambiguities.*

If the Entity spans an organisation's functional areas, then try to add definitions that would be appropriate from as many different viewpoints as possible.

It is always a good idea to review tricky definitions with stakeholders to ensure that the description works for them. This activity will often uncover shades of meaning that you were previously unaware of.

If you have had to abstract Entities from the concrete things that the operational folk deal with, then try to make sure that you include the more concrete elements as part of your description. This will help to clarify the meanings in stakeholders' minds.

Creating a Data Lexicon

I often find that it is almost impossible to record a complete picture of the data using the widely available modelling tools. This is especially true where the Entities have complex Lifecycles or Business Rules that involve many other related Entities.

Instead of trying to define complex data patterns in a data modelling tool, consider creating a Data Lexicon that can, for example, also contain images and diagrams.

Data Lexicons can help explain the Entities more thoroughly and are better suited to provide effective feedback for stakeholders.

Key Point 28   *A Data Lexicon can provide a more complete view of data, especially where it contains complex Lifecycles and/or data rules spanning Entities.*

However, as soon as you start to maintain definitions that exist beyond the core modelling tool, the question arises of how these separate definitions will be synchronised.

It might be wise to not to embark on this approach until your data model definitions have become relatively stable[13].

Entity property check-list

Obviously the name and description of the Entity are just the start in its complete definition. In addition to these, there are a number of other Entity properties that should be recorded.

When you start to define Entities, I suggest that you use the following check list to help ensure that you have recorded everything that needs to be known.

---

13   See the 'Good enough to go' section on page 222.

Property	Comments
Business and Data Rules	You will need to record the Business and Data Rules that govern the Lifecycle of each Entity. Be careful though not to stray into incorporating mechanisms and thereby defining Processes!
Data Privacy	Are there any specific implications for this data under prevailing Data Privacy legislation? For example, will your model need to be extended to include the definition of data 'owners' and access rights of the data consumers?
Regulatory Regimes	Are there any specific Regulatory or Legislative requirements to comply with, such as Financial Service regulations? These may prescribe, for example, that certain financial details about Clients need to be captured and stored, or indeed not stored. Or, for example, do organisations' or peoples' data need to be compliant with Anti-Money Laundering legislation? These additional data requirements could mean extending your models beyond what would be required purely for core operational purposes.
Governing Body Requirements	In addition to any Regulatory or Legislative constraints, many other organisations are regulated to some degree by Governing or Professional Bodies. These can have specific requirements that need to be factored into your data models. For example, they may have controls over whether People or Organisations are able to carry out certain activities. This is especially true for Medical or Legal areas, but may also be true for less obvious activities. For example, whether Electricians are suitably qualified to be able to maintain certain types of equipment.
Lifecycle	Ideally full Lifecycle details should be captured for all Entities. In other words, when and how does each instance get created, modified and finally deprecated? However, you may decide that actually the Entity Lifecycle is so simple that it is unnecessary to be fully recorded. Of particular importance to consider is whether the Entity could 'resurrect'. As an example, an employee who returns to be employed again at a later date. Chapter 14 is dedicated to this aspect of data models.

Volumes	Get a rough order of magnitude[14] as to how many of each instance is there are likely to be. Also figure into this metric the number that are 'current', 'in-flight' or 'active', compared with those that are no longer of current interest to the organisation. For example, how many of the Orders are 'active' at any point?
Retention Period	How long will the data need to be retained for each Entity? Some retention periods will be affected by regulations and statutory requirements, others purely by operational and business constraints.
CRUD Privileges	Are there any specific privileges required to Create, Read, Update or Delete this Entity data? For example, a lot of organisations have the concept of Chinese walls where one area of the business cannot see or modify the data 'belonging' to another. This may mean that you need to include ownership and access rights of different parts of internal or external organisations/individuals into your model.

---

14 For example 10, 100 or 1000 etc

5: The Characteristics Of Things
– Entities' Attributes

Introduction

We have identified Entities as representing the 'things' about which we need to record data for our organisations. In the previous chapter we discovered how to specify these, both visually, and also in terms of comprehensive definitions.

But almost every Entity will have data *characteristics* that we will need to to record about it. As a simple example, we will almost certainly want to record the Name for each Organisation.

These characteristics are the information that we exchange when describing the individual Entity occurrences with each other.

They are known as the Attributes of the Entities.

Attributes also have their own characteristics or properties that allow us to fully specify what each of them *means* and therefore what data we record for each of them.

This chapter describes the details required to specify these Attributes and also provides guidelines on how to record them in order to improve the quality of the data model.

Entity Properties - Attributes

The Entities that we specify, have properties, characteristics, or qualities that allow us to define each instance of them.

The Entity characteristics are the ones that we exchange when describing an Entity instance with each other. This is true for both inside our organisation and the external world within which the organisation operates. For example, we may exchange many details about an Order with a client who calls to discuss some aspect of it with us.

The characteristics or properties that are used to describe the Entities are called the Attributes of the Entity.

> **Key Point 29**   *Attributes are the qualities, or measurable characteristics that provide a rich and accurate understanding about each Entity occurrence.*

The data that we record about our Entities using Attributes is vitally important because it allows us to identify and qualify each of the Entity instances. In addition to this though, it allows us to record the outcomes from events that are associated with each Entity instance.

When describing an instance of our example Organisation Entity, we would need to have recorded some data about it; the immediate Attribute that springs to mind being its Name. Of course, there will be many others that we need to add to the Organisation Entity and a significant amount of the data modelling effort is spent adding well defined Attributes to each Entity.

Attributes themselves also have their own characteristics, or properties, that we need to record in our data models, so that each has a clear and unambiguous definition.

The following sections describe the characteristics that need to be recorded for the definition of each Attribute.

Attribute names

Each Attribute of an Entity needs to have its own name recorded. The Attribute names need to accurately describe the data that the Attribute contains, and so, as with Entities, careful thought needs to be given to their names.

At the Conceptual and Logical Data Model levels the name should be recorded;

- in the singular
- in plain language
- initial letter capitalised
- *absolutely not* using a systematised naming style

There is more detail in the following sections on aspects to consider when recording an Attribute's name.

Remove ambiguity from names

I am a big fan of verbose names because they reduce ambiguity and therefore make the model much easier to assimilate and agree upon.

Definitely do not abbreviate or use acronyms in Attribute names, since these can make the model more difficult to communicate and also reduce its longevity.

Standardising Attribute names

You should use a naming convention to ease the definition process and make the names consistent across your model. A commonly used naming convention is to have three potential elements to the name:

- Attribute Subject – what Entity characteristic is the data relevant to?

- Modifier – what is the Subject qualifier?

- Domain Type – which data domain is the Attribute conformed to?

For example:

Attribute Subject	Modifier	Datatype Domain	Resultant Name
Communication	Sent	Date	Communication Sent Date
Short Name			Short Name
Area		Quantity	Area Quantity
Area	Unit Of Measure	Code	Area Unit Of Measure Code

<u>No</u> technology naming conventions

The names must not use any stylistic conventions that are Technology based, such as:

- IsResponseReceived ⇨ Is Response Received

- FULL_NAME ⇨ Full Name

- Creation Datestamp ⇨ Creation Date

Instead of using 'Technologese' for the names, make them Business friendly.

Future-proof names

The Attribute names should be future-proofed and to help in this regard, they should avoid the following aspects:

- Embedded mechanisms – no 'how Processes act on the data' e.g. **Email** Sent Date ⇨ Communication Sent Date

- Organisational – no 'current organisation names or acronyms' e.g. **ABC** Unit Name ⇨ Organisation Unit Name

- Defining regimes – no 'embedded definition systems'

  e.g. Square **Metres** ⇨ Area Quantity + Area Unit Of Measure Code

No Entity name as prefix

I also suggest that you don't name the Attributes of Entities with a prefix indicating that they belong to the Entity. For example, in the Person Entity don't prefix all the Attribute names with Person:

- **Person** First Name

- **Person** Last Name

- **Person** Compliance Attainment Date

Beware also of pluralised Attribute Names. So for our Book Entity, an Attribute of 'Authors Names' should trigger alarm bells[15].

Quantities and Amounts

There are two main magnitude Attributes that recur in most data models around the globe. A typical naming convention for these is to use Quantity and Amount in the Attribute Name.

The convention typically adopted is:

- Quantity ⇨ Measurement magnitude e.g. Line Item Quantity

- Amount ⇨ Currency magnitude e.g. Payment Amount

---

15 We'll look at this in more detail in the Atomic Attributes section on page 52.

Attribute descriptions

As with Entity descriptions, once you have added an Attribute and named it, you need to add a description for it that fully defines what it represents.

As for Entity Descriptions, try to include examples that help the reader make sense of what the Attribute means. Also include under what circumstances the data would be; recorded in it, amended or removed from it.

Stale Attributes

There are many Attributes that we discover that require careful decision making. One of the key factors to consider is the accuracy of the Attribute.

As an example, only recently I was working for a client who was vitally interested in their relationships with people who were external to the organisation. Two of the things they wanted to record were the person's Job Title and Department within which they operate.

At first sight, it seems to be a valid decision, to simply add two Attributes to represent these. But what you need to consider is the way that these will be kept current. If a person leaves the external organisation, or moves to another department within it, or gets a promotion, how will that information be recorded in *your* organisation? Will there be processes that actively manage such updates? Will the information be accurate in five years from now and if not, will this matter?

What we realise is that as soon as some types of data is captured it starts to become stale and this reduces its usefulness.

Key Point 30   *Where Attributes can become Stale, the benefit of recording them at all, can be negated.*

The Data Modeller needs to consider what the shelf life of each Attribute's data is, and how it will be kept current. And possibly more importantly, is it necessary to record it at all?

Within the last few years it has become possible to track all sorts of data that was previously inconceivable.

This tells us two things:

1. It may be possible to keep all sorts of Attributes fresh now in ways that were previously inconceivable and (therefore)

2. It may be feasible to track Attributes in the near future that cannot currently be tracked

---

These preceding points are really about scope. They raise the question of whether you should include such Attributes in your data models at all.
Strangely the answer to this question may well depend on the culture of your organisation. Does it value effort being spent on the data model definitions on a continual ongoing basis? Or does it consider that the data models have been 'finished' and therefore do not require any further revisions?
If it sees creating the data model as a one-off type of activity, then it might be wise to put Attributes into your model even though it may not be possible to keep their data current today. This is so that the model has more longevity and won't need to be upgraded at some point in the future, simply because it becomes possible to harvest and record the data for these Attributes.

Dependent Attributes

Following on from the previous section about Stale Attributes, a closely related aspect for you to consider is to only record data about Base Attributes and *never* define Dependent Attributes.

So what do we mean by this?

A Dependent Attribute is one whose value depends on one or more other underlying elements of data. These elements may or may not be Attributes of the Entity.

As an example, it may be useful to record the age of something, but keeping this current as an Attribute is not a realistic option. However, it *is* realistic to record the date that each instance came into existence. So, for example, instead of recording a Person's Age, it is better to record their Date of Birth.

The Age is dependent on the instance creation date and the date at any point in time. Therefore we can calculate the Age whenever we need to, by simply carrying out some arithmetic.

Atomic Attributes

Attributes must not record data that is complex, each Attribute must represent only atomic values. This means that it cannot be made up from independent elements and cannot have any internal data structure, or pattern.

So for example, an Attribute of the Name of a Person shouldn't contain 'Teresa Green' as this is a Compound, Complex or Composite Attribute.

What these terms mean is that its data definition can be broken down into constituent parts. In the preceding case of the Person's Name Attribute, it should be represented as separate First Name and Last Name Attributes.

These constituent parts are actually the Atomic Attributes and all Attributes within your data models *must* be Atomic.

Key Point 31 **All Attributes in data models must be without any structure or internal patterns to the data they contain and these are termed Atomic Attributes.**

Be careful here though, because many stakeholders want to make Business identifiers complex. For example, patterns such as 'LC:09345/AJK' may be in common use as identifiers within your organisation.
Although the input from stakeholders for Attribute definitions is crucial, you may need to ensure that you are a <u>purist</u> in certain areas of which Atomic Attributes is definitely one. Try to avoid such structuring of Attribute data and instead probe what each element represents and try to atomicise these into separate Attributes.
Don't forget that ultimately any Atomic Attributes can always be re-combined in any implementations on UIs or reports to give a useful short hand reference for stakeholders.

Key Point 32 **In the Logical Data Model it is important to recognise that no Attributes should be complex - no matter what any future implementation may require.**

Earlier when we looked at Attribute Names, we came across a warning sign of pluralised Names such as Authors Names in our Book Entity. This Attribute obviously could not be Atomic.

So is the answer to break it up into Author 1 Name, Author 2 Name or similar?

Definitely not!

We shall come back to examine this scenario in chapter 8.

Mandatory Attributes

Some Attributes will be required, or Mandatory for each Entity instance, others will not. This book will use the Barker Notation prefix symbols as follows:

> Mandatory ➪ *

> Optional ➪ o

But when we refer to Mandatory here, what we really mean is; which Attributes *must* have values when the Entity is *first created?*

Key Point 33   *Mandatory Attributes are those Attributes that require a value when the Entity instance is first created.*

Other non-mandatory Attributes may ultimately still have data recorded for every instance of the Entity, but at a later point in the Entity's Lifecycle.

Of course there are other Attributes that will only have a low incidence of completion throughout the Entity's Lifecycle.

So really the picture is a bit more grey-scale as illustrated by figure 19.

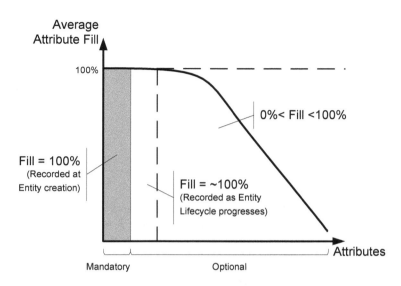

Figure 19 - Mandatory and Optional Attributes fill profile

When ordering the Attributes for an Entity you could order the Attributes in the anticipated fill proportion as shown in the schematic of figure 19. This will mean that the 'most important' ones will be ordered at the top in the tool and this may help if time is short to review and Quality Assure the model. However, you may also want to group Attributes based upon the fact that they have commonality of purpose, such as Address details. Some of the Address Attributes would be Mandatory, others have a high fill rate, others very low fill rate. But regardless of their fill percentage, you may still want to order them as per a postal delivery address.

Attribute properties - Meta Data

Attributes record the properties of the Entities, but obviously have their own characteristics that define them. We have looked at their names and descriptions, but we also need to consider other elements, one group of which is called the Attribute's Meta Data. Examples of this Meta Data include an Attribute's datatype and size.

It is important to define this Attribute Meta Data[16] so that other stakeholders can gain a complete and unambiguous understanding of the Attribute's definition[17].

16 Meta Data here refers to data definitions for the data elements themselves.

17 This Meta Data will also aid transition to any Physical Data Models that are derived from your Logical Data Model.

Attribute Datatype

Attributes should have simple datatypes defined for them such as:

- Character/String

- Number

- Date

- Boolean

- Raw

Always double check whether an Attribute's data which initially appears to be Numeric must __always__ be so, due to some inalienable law.
When deciding this, don't be persuaded by an individual being adamant that a specific Attribute must be Numeric, even if they are a key stakeholder, or SME. This opinion may be based upon a current system that the person is familiar with. However, these systems will come and go and thus such definitions may change with them.
Always remember that the Logical Data Model needs to remain immutable and agnostic to such system considerations.

However, it may be important to differentiate between Day (Date) and Intra-Day (Date and Time). This often depends on the frequency of capture of the instances and the use that will be made of the Attribute's data.

For example, if the instances are created at say monthly intervals then recording the Date at the granularity of Day (that is with no time element) may well be sufficient. But if thousands of instances are created an hour, the time element may well be quite important. In this case make sure that it is recorded as a Date *and* Time datatype.

Boolean Attributes

Another important type of Attribute to consider in your data models is a Boolean type.

This records one of two states typically 'True' or 'False'.

In all cases carefully think through whether the Attribute should be Mandatory, and is it possible that is has a default value recorded for it?

If the Attribute is not Mandatory, then it is open to question as to whether it is truly Boolean, as what would a Null represent?

Also beware that what appears as Boolean to begin with, may at a later stage contain an increasing number of values in addition to the original two states.

For example:

True, False ⇨ True, Pending, False

Quite clearly this is no longer a Boolean Attribute.

Assertion Boolean Attributes

It is worthwhile defining a convention for the name of Boolean Attributes. If they are True/False values then a common naming convention is that of an *assertion*, for example:

Is [Attribute description True] ⇨ Is Communication Sent

In many situations we are interested in the date at which such an Attribute becomes True. So using the example above, we could think about adding a second Attribute:

Communication Sent Date

Notice though that the 'Communication Sent Date' Attribute also effectively acts as a Boolean Attribute. If the Communication has not been sent, no date is recorded, but if there is a date recorded, then the Communication *has* been sent *and* we know when.

It is worthwhile examining whether this means that the True/False Attribute is in fact redundant. Do our two Attributes break the Dependent Attribute rule? However, if we only use the 'Communication Sent Date' Attribute and we know a communication was sent, but unfortunately we are not sure when, you can't reliably use the date Attribute as a replacement for the Boolean.
If the data model forms the basis for an implementation, then when making the transition from a Logical Data Model to a Physical Data Model, the Design process could decide to instantiate the Boolean and date Attributes for performance reasons. But, remember that this should not ultimately affect your decision about the Logical Data Model definition.

Attribute size

Almost all data modelling tools demand that you create lengths for the Number and Character data types. But to what level of detail is this *absolutely required* in a Logical Data Model?

This detailed analysis definitely aids the transition from a Logical Data Model to a Physical implementation. However, after years of data modelling, it slowly dawned on me that agonising about these definitions to a fine level of detail in the Logical Data Model is not justified.

For example, spending time determining whether the Organisation Name should be 28 or 30 Characters is effort that will not reap commensurate reward. Would it really have any operational significance if we recorded it as 50 Characters?

This leads to the idea of actually *qualifying* but not *quantifying* the size; that is, Small, Medium or Large would be perfectly adequate for probably the majority of the Numeric and Character Attributes.

> *Key Point 34*   *Numeric and Character Attribute sizes should be qualified but not absolutely quantified.*

The point being made here is that rather than bog down the Logical Data Model definition with this amount of detail, you might want to use a handful of rough sizes and then leave the finer detail of these definitions to any subsequent Physical Data Model activities. These (if there are any!) will be better placed to take into account, any design and implementation constraints.

Attribute Meta Data Domains

In most modelling tools it is possible to create domains as standard Meta Data definition 'templates' that you can then assign to the Attributes within your data model.

Here are some examples of Attributes Meta Data Domains and their possible definitions:

- Full Name ⇨ Character 50

- Short Name ⇨ Character 25

- Description ⇨ Character 250

- Comments ⇨ Character 4000

- Character Identifier ⇨ Character 15

- Number Identifier ⇨ Number 12

- Monetary Amount ⇨ Number 15,2

- Operational Day ⇨ Date

- Operational Intra-day ⇨ Date + Time

So now when you come to define the Organisation's Name Attribute, you can allocate the Full Name Domain definition to it and this will set its Meta Data to Character 50. Using this technique ensures a consistency across your models and will improve the quality of what you deliver.

Also, and possibly more importantly, the application of Domains allows you to stop agonising about each Attribute, and therefore shortens the Decision part of the 3-D Modelling process. This saved effort can then be better expended on other, more demanding areas.

Enhancing the Organisation Entity

We have now learned how to define each of the Attributes that in turn are used to describe the properties of our Entities. Let's use this knowledge to add some initial Attribution to our Organisation Entity.

Figure 20 shows a few first-cut Attributes added to the Organisation Entity some of which are Mandatory, others Optional.

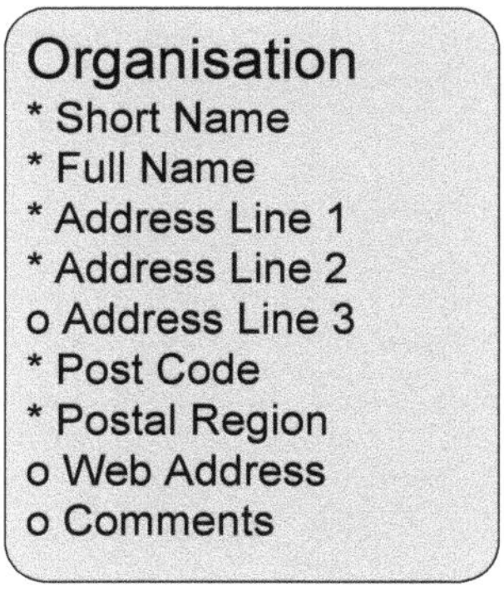

Organisation
* Short Name
* Full Name
* Address Line 1
* Address Line 2
o Address Line 3
* Post Code
* Postal Region
o Web Address
o Comments

Figure 20 – First-cut of Attribution for Organisation

Note that this is by no means the end of the story for the Organisation Entity, and we will continue to enhance it and revisit its Attributes on our journey through the book.

6: Tying Things Together
– Simple Relationships

Introduction

Entities and their Attributes can be defined in the absence of any visual representation and we certainly do not require a Logical Data Model in order to do this.

In fact, earlier we mentioned that a Data Lexicon can be used to provide a fully fleshed out definition of our Entities and this can be in the format of a document that requires no visual representation whatsoever.

So why do we need a visual data model at all?

In order to make sense of the things around us, humans invariably group things together that are alike, and create associations between these groups. We *need* to do this, so that we can build internal maps of our worlds.

If we apply this principle within the context of our organisations, in their worlds, Clients do not exist in isolation; they place Orders, they receive Products, and they make Enquiries and Payments. But how can we share the associations between the Entities that exist within our organisation's data world?

This is precisely where our Logical Data Models come into the picture.

Geographical maps rely on linking landscape elements to each other, so that we can share an understanding of these. In the same way, we need to link our Entities to each other to construct a data landscape.

Data models allow us to construct these data landscape maps that represent the *structures* of data required for our organisations to operate. More than just this representation though; it is the ability to look at the same data map as other stakeholders, and use them to *share* and *agree* the understanding of the data, that makes them so crucial.

In other words, quite literally; the way that we see the data structures and patterns, is the same way that others in the organisation see them too.

In this chapter we will add the Relationship Tool to our Toolkit. This in combination with the Entity definition Tool will allow us to construct basic Entity Relationship models.

The basic Relationship Tool that describes structures will be further enhanced so that it can define; the Business and Data Rules that these structures govern and that in turn, govern these structures.

Simple Relationships – Master Detail

We have learned how to define Entities and their Attributes, but we now need to add structures to our data models.

The structure defined in a visual data model, ties the Entities together to construct a visual map that represents our understanding of Real World data. This structural map can be shared to allow us to confirm a shared understanding of the patterns of the data with other stakeholders.

In addition, the definition of the structures and linkages specify the Data and Business Rules that govern our organisation's data.

> *Key Point 35*   *A data model is a visual representation of the definition of the <u>structure</u> of our data using a symbolic syntax.*

To create this structure relies on creating a new Tool allowing us to define the Relationships between our Entities. This tool therefore plays a pivotal role in defining the recognisable patterns in the organisation's data.

In the Real World we constantly talk of; 'One of these can include several of those', or 'This is one of those types', or 'They are located all across the country'.

> *Key Point 36*   *The <u>Relationships</u> between the Entities define the <u>structure</u> and <u>patterns</u> of the organisation's data.*

It makes no sense to have an Entity on your data model that is not related to at least one other Entity; none of our data elements can exist in isolation!

Key Point 37   *Every Entity must have at least one Relationship to another Entity on a data model.*

However, when you are at the early stages of the model's definition, the Relationships may not be at all clear. Therefore, although you may have identified an Entity, you are not yet sure how to relate it to any of the others on your data model. This is fine and expected, but as time goes on, you *must* relate it to at least one other Entity on your model, or seriously question its validity.

So far we have created a very simple example Entity of Organisation. In many organisations it is important to track to at least some degree, the relationship between this key Entity and another key Entity, that of Person. This is because for many organisations these two are central to the organisation's core activities.

Let's create an initial association between the Organisation and Person Entities to illustrate the Relationship Tool syntax. The way that we will do this is by introducing one of the commonest patterns in data modelling; that of a Master Detail Relationship.

This type of Relationship is illustrated in figure 21.

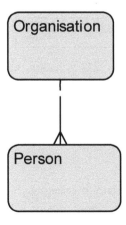

Figure 21 – Master Detail Relationship - Organisation to Person[18]

Master Detail Relationships are also commonly called Parent Child Relationships.

18   This is not a recommended model for all but the simplest cases and we will modify it to make it more sophisticated in the following chapters

Let's learn how to interpret the visual Relationship syntax in figure 21.

Relationship Syntax

To create a Relationship we use a connecting line drawn that links the two Entities[19].

These lines have their own syntax.

I am a big fan of the Barker Notation, because I think it has an intuitive and simple representation that only takes a few minutes to teach anyone.

Creating a connecting line is easy enough, so let's look at how the visual syntax of the line represents the properties of the Relationship, as depicted in figure 21, and find out what other options exist.

Relationship Optionality

Some Relationships are mandatory for an Entity and others optional.

This is shown at the *Entity connection end* of the Relationship by a continuous line for mandatory and dotted line for optional as in the following table.

Visual Syntax	Meaning for the Entity at this end of the line
_ _ _ -	Optional Relationship
_____	Mandatory Relationship

Applying this syntax to figure 21, we can read that the Relationship from Organisation to Person is optional, since the line is dotted at the Organisation end.

This means that we *may* record that an Organisation has a Person related to it, but it is *not mandatory* to associate at least one Person with each and every Organisation instance.

However, according to the data model, each Person *must* be related to an Organisation. To be clear; we *cannot* record a Person instance in the absence of relating it to an *existing* Organisation.

---

19 Or as we'll see in chapter 10, from an Entity back to itself.

Relationship Cardinality

The Cardinality of a Relationship refers to the *number* of potential Entities that are at that end of the Relationship.

The following table contains the visual syntax options for this.

Syntax	Cardinality	Number of Entities at this end of the Relationship
– – – -	0..1	Optionally none or one.
————	1	A Mandatory single Entity.
----≪	0..*	Optionally one or more, that is; none, or 1, or many.
——≪	1..*	There must be at least one.

Applying these to figure 21 we can see that there may be **one or more** People related to **one and only one** Organisation.

It is also possible to record the maximum number of Relationships that are possible, for example;

Two only ⇨ ——²≪

I cannot remember the last time I have used this syntax though, and before recording it in your data model, you need to ask whether this number is constrained by some rule that is absolutely *immutable*. For example, each Person must have two and only two biological parents[20].

Relationship Type frequencies

In my experience, the Relationship patterns do not have a uniform distribution; some are very common and some are quite rare.

In addition, there are some that I don't believe can or should exist!

The following table summarises the combinations and the relative frequencies based upon my experience.

---

20 Even this seemingly inviolate law of nature has been overturned by recent advances in medical techniques.

Relationship Type (Shorthand notation)	Frequency	Comments
– – – – – – (1:1) — – – – – –⎯ (1:1) — ⎯⎯⎯⎯ (1:1)	0%	Although valid in certain High Level data models and at the beginning of the Discover process, these Relationships probably indicate a lack of Abstraction.
– – – – –< (1:M)	Low	Rare because the Detail Entity does not need to be related to the Master Entity.
– – ⎯⎯< (1:M)	>95%	This Relationship predominates in all of my Normalised models.
⎯⎯⎯⎯< (1:M)	Low	This means that at least one Detail Entity instance must be recorded at the same time as the Master Entity instance, for example an Order must have at least one Order Item on it.
>--------< (M:M)	90% in High Level data models.	Common in Conceptual and initial Logical cuts. Must be resolved in the Logical Data Model.
>------⎯< (M:M)	0% in Logical	
>⎯⎯⎯< (M:M)	Extremely rare even in High Level data models. 0% in Logical	

So far in our description of the Relationship between Organisations and People, we have described the Optionality and Cardinality, but not what the Relationship *represents*.

In other words; we haven't yet defined its *meaning!*

Obviously this is not acceptable since, as we know, the data's meaning is everything.

Defining Relationships

We need to define the Relationships in some detail because they determine the structure and patterns of our data. The elements to define are described in the following sections.

Relationship names

In order to introduce rigour, Relationships should have names created that describe what they represent. This name should contain a *concise* description that is displayed in the data model and is constructed using a verb.

Richard Barker suggested that the Relationship should be named in both directions. The best way to try to describe the naming convention is to use our Master Detail Relationship as an example:

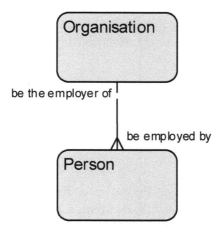

Figure 22 – Defining Master Detail Relationship names

Here is the way to read the syntax in the model fragment contained in figure 22.

'Each'	[Starting Entity]	[Starting Optionality]	[Starting Relationship descriptor]	[Ending Cardinality]	[Ending Entity]
Each	Organisation	may	be the employer of	one or more	People
Each	Person	must	be employed by	one and only one	Organisation

Figure 23 shows how to read the Relationship visually from the Organisation Entity perspective of the Relationship.

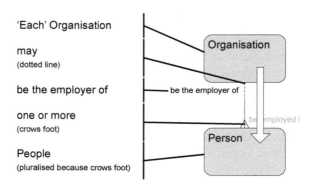

'Each' Organisation

may
(dotted line)

be the employer of

one or more
(crows foot)

People
(pluralised because crows foot)

be the employer of

be employed i

Organisation

Person

Figure 23 – Reading a Relationship

Relationship definitions

In addition to the name, more detail needs to be recorded about the Business and Data Rules governing how the Relationship gets created, modified and ultimately removed.

Here are a couple of examples to give you the flavour of the kinds of details to be included in the full definition of a Relationship[21].

'After negotiations have taken place and the Sub-contractor has formally agreed to the Terms and Conditions, they can be associated with the Service Level Agreement'

'At any time within the 'Notice Period' specified in the specific Terms and Conditions of the Service Level Agreement, a Sub-contractor can terminate their inclusion to provide services under the Service Level Agreement'

Some pragmatic modelling tips

Over the years I have found a couple of Richard Barker's original standards and guidelines caused some practical issues and I have adapted them to remove these.

In terms of the requirement to name the Relationships reading both ways, I often found myself spending many hours restating the Relationship on the data models in both directions using the preceding pattern. But I started to become increasingly uneasy about doing so.

My disquiet grew due to the extra time and maintenance effort that only rarely seemed to add any further understanding to the model. In almost all cases, the

---

21 Don't forget though that ideally these definitions should not make reference to any mechanistic constraints.

inverse definition for any given Relationship definition, did not contribute any additional understanding to the model, because it was self-evident from the first Relationship description.

Apart from the wasted time and effort, for me the final nail in the coffin for this convention, was simply the amount of space taken up on the model. As a result of recording the Relationship descriptions at both ends, the text in many models became crowded and its position often made it unclear about which Relationship it was the description for.

This had the effect of making the data models *less* legible and increasing their ambiguity – the very opposite of the intention!

Another deviation that I have made due to years of experience, has been to drop the verb from the description unless there is any ambiguity about it. Again this is in the interests of saving space and improving the model's legibility.

The vast majority of the verbs contained in the descriptions of my models were either 'be' or possessive e.g. 'has', 'have'. Because of this, I have tended to assume that the reader of the Relationship will insert the correct verb part of the Relationship definition naturally and deterministically, simply to make it grammatically correct.

So for example:

[be the] employer of ⇨ employer of

[be] employed by ⇨ employed by

You will notice that I have used this technique throughout the book. Strictly speaking though, you *should* use the full description including the verb to avoid ambiguity. However, if like me you find that actually it doesn't add any real value but soaks up valuable space on your models, then you may wish to omit it from any Relationship definitions that don't *require* it.

Relationship Transferability

One of the features of the Barker Relationships is that they are transferrable. Figure 24 indicates that a Facility Resource Booking can be transferred from one Person to another.

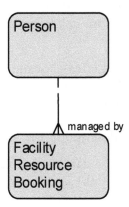

Figure 24 - Relationship transfer example

In my experience, this reading of the Relationship is not at the forefront of most Data Modellers' minds.

Barker introduced the diamond symbol to indicate that the Relationship is *not* transferrable as illustrated in figure 25.

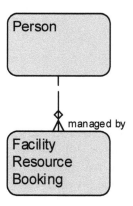

Figure 25 - Relationship transfer *not* allowed

This diamond indicates that the management of a Facility Resource Booking *cannot* be transferred from one Person to another.

If a relationship cannot be transferred from one Master Entity instance to another then this (non) Transfer property needs to be recorded for it.

For most situations it is fine for the Relationship to be transferrable. If we just look at this particular case for a moment; if, for example, the original Person is on annual leave or leaves the organisation altogether, it seems reasonable that someone else could have the management of the Facility Resource Booking transferred to them.

But be careful!

This implicit transferability is a double edged sword, since once the transfer has taken place, the data model will not provide any way of telling who previously managed the booking. This is something that is often not taken into account, but you need to be aware of it. Should this previous Relationship need to be tracked, then a different approach to the model will need to be adopted.

Of course, if the model is ultimately implemented, then we could make use of an audit capability in an implemented system. But we must not factor that consideration into our Logical Data Model definition. If the organisation needs to know the Person Facility Resource Booking history[22], then this should be represented in the Logical Data Model data structures.

But there is a simpler resolution to these multiple Relationships that could exist between the same two Entity instances. It is one that we will describe in the following Many to Many Relationships section.

Multiple Relationships Between Two Entities

Of course, it is possible to have more than one parallel[23] Relationship between the same two Entities as illustrated in figure 26.

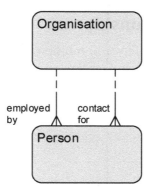

Figure 26 - Multiple Parallel Relationships

---

22   This theme is picked up in much more detail in chapter 14 which looks at Lifecycles in our models.

23   By 'parallel Relationships', we refer to them being between the same two Entities and having the same Master Detail 'direction'.

This model fragment indicates that there is more than one Relationship definition that can exist between an Organisation and a Person. In this simple example there is one Relationship definition that indicates the Organisation that employs each Person and another that indicates one or more People can act as a point of contact for an Organisation.

Whilst this is a perfectly valid feature in a data model, be warned that these repeated parallel Relationships may give a clue that a Many to Many Relationship is required, as described in the next section.

> ***Key Point 38***   ***Multiple parallel Relationships between two Entities may indicate that a Many to Many Relationship is required.***

If you are not totally sure about whether there may be more parallel Relationship definitions that will come to light in the future, you may be wise to combine the Relationships as a single Many to Many Relationship.

However, where there is low or no risk of more such Relationships coming to light in the future, modelling it as a Many to Many Relationship loses some of the explicit rigour of your data model definition[24].

Many To Many Relationships

Both Relationship transferability and multiple parallel Relationships between two Entities may indicate that in fact there are Many to Many Relationships[25] that exist between them.

Figure 27 illustrates a possible remodelling of the preceding examples.

---

24   We will pick this theme up again in chapter 12.
25   For Many to Many Relationships we will use a shorthand notation of M:M Relationships henceforth.

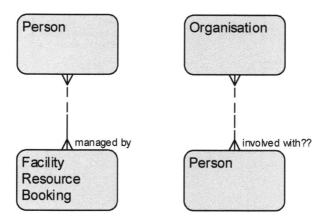

Figure 27 – M:M Relationships

This M:M Relationship Type occurs frequently at the start of the modelling process. Whilst they are perfectly acceptable in high level models, as we refine our Logical Data Models, these Relationships will require your attention and need to be resolved into more tightly defined Relationships.

Notice also that in the example in figure 27, the definition 'involved with' of Person to Organisation is so ill defined[26] that it tells us straight away that this is an area for further analysis.

Resolving Many to Many Relationships

M:M Relationships in our models indicate that there is potentially more than one Relationship between the same the two occurrences in two Entities. For example, the same Person and the same Organisation can have multiple Relationships between them. We need to record which Relationship occurrences are which and of course in Entity Relationship modelling, we use Entities to record data. This means that we need to introduce an *Entity to record each of the Relationship instances*.

The resolution of the M:M Relationship produces a standard pattern as illustrated in figure 28.

---

26   It may as well say 'is related to'!

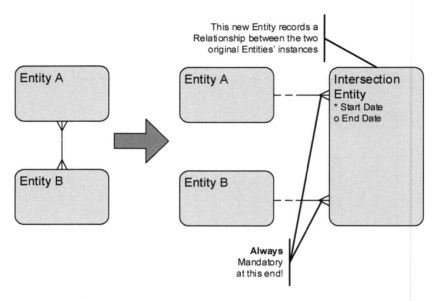

Figure 28 – Resolution of M:M Relationships

Often the Entity type used in the resolution of M:M Relationships is called an Intersection Entity.

> **Key Point 39**   *Intersection Entities are used to resolve M:M Relationships by recording the instances of the Relationships that exist between the two original Entities.*

Notice that because the new Intersection Entity records the instance of a Relationship between the other two Entities, neither of its own Relationships can be optional. This is *irrespective* of the original M:M Relationship's optionality definitions!

> **Key Point 40**   *An Intersection Entities Relationships to the original M:M Relationship Master Entities, __must be Mandatory__ irrespective of the original M:M Relationships' Optionality.*

Notice also that in figure 28 the new Intersection Entity's Relationships are

Many to One from its perspective. However, this need not always be the case since each of these may in turn be M:M Relationships. This is not a common resolution outcome, but you should always probe these newly defined Relationships with some care to ensure that they are indeed correct.

Another typical part of the pattern is the addition of Date Attributes to the new Intersection Entity. In many cases it is important to record when the Relationship is created and when it becomes no longer relevant, hence we typically add Attributes to record these dates.

So applying our standard pattern as in figure 28 to the M:M Relationships between Organisation and Person in figure 27, we produce this model fragment.

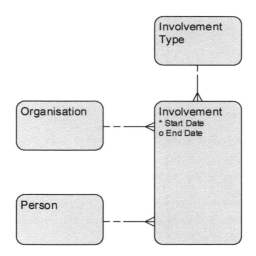

Figure 29 – Resolution of Organisation to Person M:M Relationships

This is not the end game of the resolution of M:M Relationships and we will add further features to our resolution Tool again in chapter 9.

Master Detail With Detail group

Another commonly encountered Relationship pattern is where there is a Master Detail pair of Entities with an additional Entity that exists between them[27].

Figure 30 illustrates this with an example using our simple Organisation and Person model we created earlier.

---

27 Notice that if the layout is not clear and drawn as suggested in chapter 2 in the Splatter-gram section, it is very hard to spot these structural patterns.

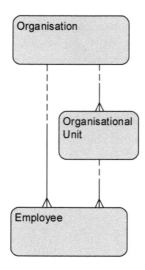

Figure 30 - Master Detail with Detail Group

This intervening Entity often represents a grouping of the Detail Entity within the context of the Master Entity.

In the model fragment of figure 30, we see that a Person *must* be associated with not only an Organisation, but also an Organisational Unit. This Organisational Unit *must* in turn also be associated with an Organisation.

At first sight this all seems fine, but this is a pattern that always sets alarm bells ringing for me, and I always devote some effort seeing if it is genuinely accurate and if so, what it *actually* represents.

The question is; why are there two possible ways that the Person and the Organisation Entities are related? Of course, these two ways to link People and Organisations *could* be valid for any number of reasons.

However, the first check I would want to carry out, would be to test for a potential Relationship redundancy.

Redundant Relationship

If a Person *must* be employed within an Organisational Unit that itself *must* be defined within one and only one Organisation, it is possible that the direct Relationship between Organisation and Person is redundant. What we mean by this is that as soon as the Person is associated with the Organisational Unit, they are implicitly also associated to the same Organisation as it is.

Let's imagine that in this case there is no requirement for the additional

Relationship. Removing it also removes any possible risks of inconsistent data relationships.

If the direct Relationship is redundant between the Person and the Organisational Unit then a better representation is illustrated in figure 31.

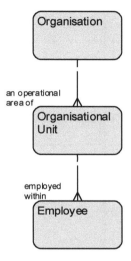

Figure 31 – Redundancy Removed

If the Relationships do not exhibit redundancy, then other common patterns for the Relationships from the Employee Entity to its Master Entities in this model include:

- they are both Optional

- only one is Optional

Possible definitions that illustrate these patterns are described in the following sections.

Both Relationships are Optional

If we want to record the Employees for both our own organisation and those of other organisations, then it makes sense to model both of the Relationships and make them optional.

This is because, for Employees that are external to our Organisation, we don't necessarily know the association of the Employee to *their* Organisation's *internal* structures. Even if we could know this, it is highly unlikely that we would want to try to track the Relationship over time[28].

---

28   For the same reasons as were argued for Stale Attributes on page 51.

This means that the Relationship from the *external* Employee to *its* employing Organisation would need to be mandatory, but that the Relationship between the *external* Employee and the *internal* Organisation Unit needs to be optional.

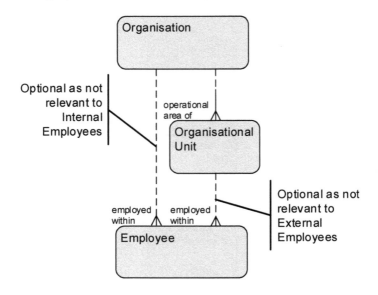

Figure 32 – Optional Master Detail with Optional Detail Group

However, if we need to track the Organisational Unit within which all *internal* Employees operate, then we only need to record the association of these Employees to an Organisation Unit. We know that this in turn is defined by being associated with a single Organisation, the host Organisation. But the Relationship between the *internal* Employee and an Organisation is not required and so it also needs to be optional.

This means that both Relationships must be optional as shown in figure 32.

One Relationship is Optional– temporal effect

A possible interpretation of the model in figure 30 is that we *must* associate the Employees with an employing Organisation. But what if we don't know which Organisational Unit they are associated with at the time of capture of their details?

We will only be able to record this Relationship it when it becomes known to us and therefore it needs to be optional.

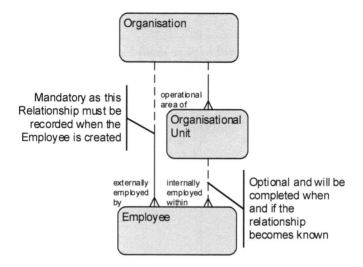

Figure 33 – Mandatory Master Detail with Optional Detail Group

Figure 33 illustrates a model that represents this scenario.

We could fill many more pages with the possible options for why the alternate Relationship paths exist. The point to make here is that you must be able to spot these and spend time validating their existence. This needs to be a part of the quality assurance of your model and a technique for doing this is covered in chapter 18.

Methodical Data Model Layout

In chapter 2 we discovered the importance of the communication purpose of our data models. We saw how Splattergrams obscure a data model's meaning rather than facilitate it.

Now we know in a bit more detail about Relationships, we need to enhance the layout guidelines for data models.

I would *strongly* urge you to adopt a methodical layout that can yield significant extra benefits from our models.

To achieve these benefits, I recommend that a layout is used that places the

Many end of all Relationships towards the right or bottom[29] of data models[30].

Always adopt a methodical layout to your models and place the Many ends of the Relationship to the right and bottom of the model.

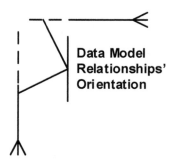

Figure 34 - Data Model Relationship orientation

Once this style is adopted, data models actually reveal several important characteristics, as illustrated in figure 35.

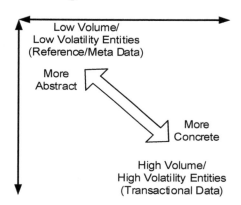

Figure 35 - Revealed patterns in data models

For example, at a glance we can see which are the:

- high volume Entities and

- candidate Reference Data

---

29 Again this is a slight deviation from Barker's original idea that the crow's feet should point up and to the left – the so-called 'dead crow's feet'. I find that it is more intuitive to have them pointing down and to the right, as this fits with the concept of Master Detail that we are familiar with.

30 This convention is especially relevant to Normalised Logical Data Models and Physical Data Models.

Once you take the effort required to methodically and consistently lay out your data models, something really weird happens.

At some point in their development small children learn to start reading rapidly, using pattern matching techniques, and stop reading words letter by letter.

In the same way you will notice that to gain an understanding of the model, you will no longer have to trace your finger around it, mouthing the Entity and Relationship names! Instead, you will immediately have the gist of the model and begin to spot structural patterns within seconds.

In other words, you will be able to start to understand and Quality Assure data models rapidly and in ways previously impossible!

Okay, this may sound a bit like a crazy money-back type of promotion, but I challenge you to try it!

Name Guidelines Summary

At several points in the book so far we have acquired guidelines of the way to define the names of Entities, Attributes and Relationships. Given their importance, this section recaps these for clarity.

Abstracting names

We learned at the beginning of this book that data provides a way of measuring and describing what is happening in the Real World. It is important to remember though, that good data models require the application of abstraction to ensure their longevity and future-proofing. One simple aspect of abstracting that is often overlooked is that of abstracting the names of Entities, Attributes and definitions of Relationships.

So let's spend a moment to review the role of abstraction on name definitions.

Often the initial choice of names reflects the way things are currently carried out and therefore can be highly mechanistic. This may arise as a consequence of using Process definitions as the source of our understanding, rather than abstracted Functions.

Earlier in the book, we discovered that removing *any* mechanistic or restrictive references from names used in data models, improves the future-proof qualities of data models.

> **Key Point 41** **Abstracting Names for Entities, Attributes and Relationships helps to improve their longevity and makes them more resilient to any organisational Process changes.**

For example, Lease, Sale and Management Contract are all types of Legal Agreements. Everyone in the organisation may only think about these three types and indeed the organisation may be split along the separate types as Business Lines. However, as a Data Modeller you may want to consider abstracting these into a single Legal Agreement Entity.
The Data Modeller needs to question the basis of every name used in data models and, wherever possible, abstract them. This will result in the models being more resilient to future Operational changes. Partly this can be achieved by simply removing any mechanistic references from them.

Synonyms

Synonyms refer to the different names that may be used to describe the same Entities, Attributes or parts of Relationship definitions within an organisation.

We have already encountered two potentially conflicting imperatives that will try to pull your definitions in different directions:

1. Communication clarity

2. Abstraction

Synonyms can help to bridge the gap that can be caused by these opposing forces. It can help to provide understanding of an abstracted name by providing more concrete names that stakeholders would be able to identify with ease.

Also when Entities span different Business areas it can be helpful to have Synonyms recorded to help remove any divisions in understanding caused by the stakeholders who have differing operational experience.

Therefore it is critical to record these in data models to help align *every* stakeholder's understanding of it.

Where different parts of an organisation have different interpretations, it is important for the Data Modeller to collate and define the different terms and include as many as possible within the Entity, Attribute and Relationship definitions. This allows the meaning of definitions to be accessible for as many parts of the organisation as possible.

7: Which One Is It?
– Identifying Entities

Introduction

The scourge of duplicate data within an organisation can be quite debilitating for it. It can result in a significant amount of wasted effort, money and potentially, even reputational loss.

In my opinion, one of the hardest challenges in data modelling is that of building defences against duplicate instances of its Entities.

Maybe because of this, many data models that I see, completely ignore this challenge. Instead of tackling the issue, a Numeric Identifier Attribute is systematically added to every Entity in the belief that this has somehow solved the problem.

However, simply adding an Identifier Attribute is *avoiding the question*, not *providing an answer*. And as a consequence, it is potentially storing up problems for any subsequent implementations that make use of the data model.

Therefore, as we develop our data models, we must build into them the ability to uniquely identify the individual occurrences of each Entity. This crucial information can have many practical applications, for example, for Data Quality framework definitions, or Data Migration projects, and hence provide real benefit to the organisation.

This chapter describes the problem in more detail and then makes use of Attributes as a new Tool to help us uniquely identify each instance in their Entities. The criteria for suitability of Attributes and syntax required to create this new Tool are described so that we can add it to our growing Toolkit.

Unique Identifier Attributes

When we carry out operational activities that relate to one of our Entities' occurrences, how do we make sure that we are referencing the right one? In other words, how do we tell the instances of each Entity one from another?

For example, when discussing a **Client** who just enquired about a **Product** on their last **Order**, how do we know the identity of the highlighted Entities so we can respond to the enquiry?

If we don't tackle this issue in our Logical Data Models, we are potentially storing up duplicate data problems in our data landscape.

If ignored, this duplicate data problem can cause:

- implementation delays and increased costs

- Data Quality issues – particularly impacting reporting

- lack of consistency when exchanging data between systems

- difficulties in Data Migrations

- degradation in your clients' experience and confidence

Defining the uniqueness of an Entity can be a very tricky question to answer for many of the key ones in most data models.

If we were to go to any of the operational areas in our organisation to ask how they tell the instances apart, we might find that the answer is reliant on the knowledge of the people who work with the data day in and day out.

This would almost certainly be the case if the number of instances is low, for example, if the organisation has a small number of stable Clients and these are widely known in operational areas.

But this does not provide a systematic solution. Nor does it work when there are potentially millions of occurrences such as Clients of an Energy Provider, or a Bank. So, how do we solve the problem of being able to unequivocally identify each individual occurrence for each of our Entities?

The property of an Entity that allows each instance to be differentiated from the others is called its Unique Identifier.

We have already seen that Attributes are the characteristics of our Entities that we can use to describe each instance. They therefore make a natural choice to use to *identify* each instance of our Entities.[31]

Key Point 42   ***Every single instance of an Entity needs to have its uniqueness guaranteed using a Unique Identifier and this can be based upon one or more of its Attributes.*** [30]

---

31   In chapter 9 we'll extend our Tools to include Relationships that can also be used to form part of the Unique Identifier.

Defining Unique Identifier Attributes

When assessing their suitability to define your Unique Identifier, there are some characteristics of any candidate Attributes that you need to take into account.

The Attributes that are used in the Unique Identifier *must*:

- be Mandatory – the Attribute *must* have a value at the time the Entity is *recorded*

- adhere to all of the normal rules for Attribute definition and in particular:

  o be Atomic[32] – has no internal structure

  o not be Dependent – is *not* dependent on other underlying data elements

- be Stable[33] – its values cannot change over time

Unique Identifier syntax

Once we have established the Attributes that will be used to create the Unique Identifier, the syntax to indicate that they are Unique Identifier Attributes is the easy bit.

In Barker notation any Unique Identifier Attributes should be prefixed with a '**#**'.

For example:

> # Registration Number

> # Order Number

Selecting Valid Unique Identifier Attributes

In a lot of models that I see, a Numeric Attribute has been added to the Entity as the Unique Identifier. This is often carried out methodically and with no further thought being given to the issue of Real World uniqueness.

But this approach is simply side-stepping the underlying question.

For why this doesn't really help, look at some example rows for a Person Entity in figure 36.

---

32   For more about this characteristic, see page 52.
33   This is a topic we will revisit later on page 90.

Person Identifier	First Name	Last Name
123	Dave	Knifton
321	Dave	Knifton

Figure 36 – Are these People duplicates?

Oh dear! Is it really a duplicate? How can we tell?

Obviously adding a standard Numeric Identifier as the Unique Identifier without considering what it means, is not the right answer. In the following sections we will consider what the other options are.

Natural Keys

What we mean by Natural Keys are Unique Identifiers that are based upon one or more Real World Attributes of the Entity. That is, Attributes that are *intrinsically* part of the definition of each instance in the Real World.

Key Point 43   *Natural Keys are ideal candidates to be the Unique Identifier for any Entity, because they occur as part of the definition of the Entity in the Real World.*

Wherever possible, Natural Keys should trump any other candidates to become the Unique Identifiers.

Sometimes this point is overlooked and you may hear, for example, a 'Client Reference' being described as a Natural Key. Whilst it might be a good Unique Identifier, it is certainly not a Natural Key and therefore needs some further thought before being adopted.

The questioning required revolves around whether the Client Reference is actually *intrinsically* a part of the Client's definition in the Real World? Certainly this is not the case.

External Organisations or People are extremely unlikely to have a handy Client Reference Natural Key that can be used to universally identify them.

If only!

Typically, this Attribute has been added by *internal* operational people to act as a shorthand reference they can use to identify which Client it is that they are discussing.

Because it is not a Natural Key, it is not the best choice as a Unique Identifier, since the same Organisation can be assigned two different Client References. In fact, in the absence of being able to recognise that it *is* the same Organisation, it is *highly likely* that the same external entity *will* be allocated two or more different Client References over time.

What would prevent this? Certainly the Client Reference will offer no defence against this happening.

Unfortunately, Natural Keys are not nearly as abundant as you might hope for in the Real World. Doubly unfortunately for Data Modellers, this is especially true in the case of People and Organisations.

Creating a Natural Key Unique Identifier

So let's try to find a Unique Identifier for a Person Entity. We'll try to use a Natural Key as our starting point.

In the Real World we tend to know people by their names and so this seems to provide a good start. Figure 37 illustrates our first-cut of the Unique Identifier for the Person Entity.

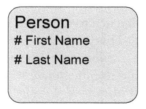

Figure 37 – A first-cut Person Unique Identifier

In this example we have used two Attributes 'First Name' and 'Last Name' as our Unique Identifier.

Where two or more Attributes are used to form the Unique Identifier it is known as a Compound Unique Identifier or Compound Key.

But of course, it doesn't take a very big sample size before we bump into duplicates of people using only these two Attributes. So we need to add something else.

An obvious Attribute to consider would be the 'Date Of Birth'.

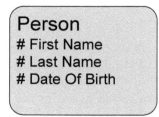

Figure 38 – An improved Person Unique Identifier

This works quite well, again up to another threshold of sample size. But it has one significant problem and that is that people tend to name their children with names that are popular at the date of their birth!

This means that human behaviour tends to introduce a lot more duplicates than purely random allocation would create. Unfortunately for us, this swarm behaviour is prevalent in many aspects of human activities, and so affects a wide range of Attributes that we may wish to use as our Natural Keys.

There is also a more fundamental problem and that is that people are extremely unlikely to want to divulge their *actual* Date of Birth just to become a Client! Of course for some organisations this problem is not as significant because they must collect sufficient data about the people they deal with to satisfy Anti Money Laundering legislation.

But even an organisation's diligence to comply with such legal and regulatory constraints is not fool-proof. This is because establishing compliance relies on various combinations of evidence to be provided by the Client. This allows legal entities, who have the incentive, to use different combinations and thereby become different instances!

So it is hard to find a good Unique Identifier for a Person Entity using Natural Keys; let's see if it is any easier for an Organisation Entity.

Initially the Name may look to be a good candidate to identify each instance of the Organisation Entity. But there are many good reasons why this is not the case, including that an organisation may:

- change its name over time
- simply use a trading name and actually be another organisation altogether
- be incorrectly captured initially

In the same way that we have difficulty to uniquely identify people using a

Natural Key, for the Organisation Entity we can quickly see that we also have difficulty in creating a Natural Key to use as its Unique Identifier.

Externally mastered Unique Identifiers

If Natural Keys are not available for your Entity then the next best approach is to adopt an external referencing system that can be used to master the Unique Identifier. In some respects these are *almost* Natural Keys when considered by our internal operation's perspective.

For example:

- Tax Number

- An ISO Code

- Anatomical Therapeutic Classification

- Standard Industry Code

But we must be careful here and always check whether the Attribute/s are mastered by an appropriate authority.

In particular before adopting an externally mastered key consider the following:

1. Is it a stable allocation or could the mastering authority reallocate codes[34]?

2. Is the organisation behind it in for the long haul?

3. Does the organisation have full coverage for all of your Entity's scope?

Only if the answers to these questions are a resounding 'Yes' can you feel confident to use it in your model.

If we look at the very simple example of the Book Entity that we saw in chapter 4, it is relatively easy to use an externally mastered key Attribute for it. This is the 13 character ISBN identifier which is more constant than even the Book's title[35]. Each Book receives an ISBN prior to publication that is ultimately governed by an international body.

---

34 A good example of a changing set of definition codes is the externally mastered International Standard Industrial Classification (ISIC) codes that got updated to Revision 4 in 2008.

35 However, it is only guaranteed to identify the book in a given format. If the same 'book' is published as an e-book then it is allocated a different ISBN!

Figure 39 – An externally mastered Unique Identifier Attribute

However this tends to be the exception.

The externally mastered key works well for Books, but what about our more demanding Organisation Entity?

If the occurrences of the Organisations in which we are interested are all Companies, then it would be appropriate to use the following model where the Company registration is controlled by a relevant authority within the jurisdiction of your model's scope. For example in the UK this would be Companies House.

Figure 40 shows this modification to our Organisation Entity to use this externally mastered Registration Number.

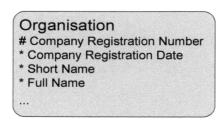

Figure 40 – Organisation Company Unique Identifier

The following table shows some sample data that this model supports.

Company Registration Number	Short Name
1234567	Supernova Industries
4567328	FutureAnalytics Ltd
6543216	Retro Interiors Design

External Unique Identifier Domains

There is however a problem that arises from our use of the 'Company Registration Number' as the Unique Identifier for the Organisation.

In the example illustrated in figure 40, the Organisation Entity is uniquely identified by a Company Registration number. This means that any Organisation that is not a Company cannot be recorded!

We therefore need to introduce the ability to record the regime that masters the Registration Numbers. This becomes especially important for global data models, since it is highly likely that there will be at least one mastering authority per jurisdiction.

Therefore we need to remodel the Organisation Entity to be able to record the Registration regime that mastered the Registration Number. This will immediately allow us to support, for example, a Registered Charity or an Educational Institution.

To indicate the Registration Authority we'll add a 'Registration Authority Name' Attribute to create a Compound Unique Identifier as illustrated in figure 41.

Organisation
\# Registration Number
\# Registration Body Name
* Registration Date
* Short Name
* Full Name
...

Figure 41 – Organisation compound Unique Identifier

This means that although the Registration Number is not guaranteed to be unique in itself, it *will* be unique in combination with its Registration Authority Name.

Let's see what the sample data would look like for this model.

Registration Number	Registration Authority Name	Short Name
123456	Companies House	Supernova Industries
456732	Companies House	FutureAnalytics Ltd
654321	Companys House	Retro Interiors Design
654321	Educational Institution	St Bartholomew Academy

Figure 42 – Example Organisation Unique Identifier data

This capability to record the external mastering regime is an important pattern that needs to be built into your models whenever the Unique Identifier is externally mastered.

Key Point 44 **Where the Unique Identifier relies on one or more externally mastered Attributes, the mastering authority for these should also be incorporated into the model.**

Internally mastered Unique Identifiers

There is something else to think about here and that is; if no Natural Key Attribute, or effective external mastering is feasible, then maybe you can use a Master Data Management approach to provide the Unique Identifier. This relies upon your organisation carrying out due diligence processes and then allocating a Master Data Key to each instance.

So, for example, a simple ratification workflow could mean that all Client Reference Identifiers are ratified as part of your Master Data Management. This is not a purist answer, but unfortunately may well be the best that can be achieved for certain of your Entities.

If there are potentially millions of instances of the Entity then this is not a realistic option as the effort involved would exceed the relative worth of uniquely identifying each instance.

Alternate Keys

It is hard to find strong candidates for the Unique Identifiers for Entities. Sometimes though, you can be blessed with not only having a reliable Unique Identifier, but also one or more Attribute/s that could be used to define a second Unique Identifier. This is termed an Alternate Key.

In our first-cut of the Unique Identifier using Natural Keys, we considered Attributes that we may have subsequently rejected as Unique Identifier candidates. In the case of our Organisation Entity for example, we examined whether the Organisation Name Attribute could be a good Unique Identifier. After some consideration we may have decided it was not stable enough to use as a Unique Identifier.

However, these first-cut Keys can still have a role to play in identifying the instances. Sometimes they form good candidates for Alternate Keys.

The Attributes for an Alternate Key must ideally possess the same characteristics that were listed for the Unique Attributes on page 87.

Descriptors

Descriptors are one or more Attributes that allow easy recognition of each instance of an Entity, particularly by the operational people in your organisation. Alternate Keys are very good as acting as Descriptors. For many of our Entities this may be in the form of the name of the instance.

If we get a call from 'Supernova' how will they be recognised?

It is highly likely that the person on the other end of the call would know their Organisation's Name, but would be less likely to be able to provide us with their Organisation Registration Number. Therefore the Organisation Name would make a good Descriptor.

Surrogate Keys

Whilst we are looking at the Keys used to uniquely identify the instances of our Entity, it is worth mentioning Surrogate Keys. These Keys typically use a Number type Attribute to define the Unique Identifier.

It was suggested earlier in this chapter that the *methodical* addition of these to *every* Entity masks the problem of identifying each occurrence, and certainly does not in itself provide a universal solution.

However, there is a place for Surrogate Keys in Logical Data Models. To my mind, however, they are only relevant where the organisation has total control over the identification for each instance of the Entity.

> **Key Point 45** **Surrogate Keys have a place to play in uniquely identifying Entities, but only where the _definition of the Entity instance is under the total control of your organisation_.**

Internally Mastered Reference Data

Internally Mastered Reference Data is defined purely within the organisation based upon its own view of the world.

If we need a Customer Discount Level Entity to have some ratified values in it, we can define and maintain this Domain _wholly within the organisation_. Since we control the unique identity of each Entity instance ourselves, we can allocate a Surrogate Key for it.

However, using an internally generated People Number as a Surrogate Key is not a valid candidate as a Unique Identifier. This is because the organisation does not control the creation of People; they exist in the absence of our organisation, and were created by processes beyond the control of our organisation.

Imagine for a second asking a caller whether they are 'Person 987654?'

Hence, in the case of the Person Entity a Surrogate Key should not be used as a Unique Identifier.

Although according to the Surrogate Key, these instances are clearly uniquely identified, the Surrogate Keys still do not allow us to answer the question; are the instances unique?[36]

Internally Mastered Transactional Data

Since we create Transactional data within the operations of our organisations the allocation of Surrogate Keys for these kinds of Entities is perfectly valid. So, for example, it is quite valid for us to allocate an Order Number as a Unique Identifier to the Order instances.

In fact, there are a wide range of these Transactional Entities for which this is an acceptable approach. However, when discussing operational details with our Clients, we need to think about how _they_ would identify the instance. Will we constantly require them to be able to quote _our_ internal reference such as their Subscription Account Number?

---

36   Refer back to figure 36 on page 88 to help visualise this question.

Therefore we would almost certainly need to also consider Alternate Keys that would be more externally facing. As an example, creating a Payment Reference might well be a good Unique Identifier that we allocate internally. But when a Client enquires about a payment they made, we need to consider carefully how we would be able to identify each payment from their perspective.

Part of this identification might be to recognise that the payment was *related* to the Client. We will see how Relationships can help to create Unique Identifiers in chapter 9.

8: Attributes That Become Entities – Normalisation

Introduction

So far we have added the following core Tools into our Toolkit; Entities and their Attributes, and the Relationships that bind them together. We learned that Attributes record the defining characteristics of our Entities and some can, at least partially, help us to uniquely identify each occurrence of each Entity.

As we start to add more detail to our Attribute definitions though, we notice that the way some of them relate to the Entity in which we initially defined them, does not quite 'fit'.

These 'ill-fitting' Attributes raise questions about the data model structure, which in turn requires us to use a technique called Normalisation.

I often get asked to explain this technique and there are plenty of definitions of Normalisation readily available. Although these definitions make sense *after* you understand Normalisation, I have never been convinced that they provide an easy path for people to learn about the process in the first place.

What they definitely do provide though, are easy to remember phrases describing Normalisation that can be useful in discussions when checking that a data model has a sound structural state.

What we'll describe in this chapter is the way that Normalisation is required from a data model development perspective. We'll do this by answering the following two questions;

1. What are the symptoms that make you realise Normalisation is required?

2. What patterns can we add to our Toolkit to carry out Normalisation?

When we talk about Normalisation we need to also be aware that there are several levels of it; the one most commonly called Normalisation is actually 'Third Normal Form'. It is this level that forms the basis for the Normalisation Tools that we will add to our Toolkit.

When Attributes Demand Their Own Entities

As we start to think more carefully about our Attributes, and in particular how they vary with each instance of the Entity that they describe, we notice that some of them don't really 'belong' to the Entity in which we initially created them.

This gives rise to a problem, the resolution of which is a technique called Normalisation.

We've already mentioned Normalised models a few times without attempting to define exactly what this term means. However, to describe operational data accurately, we must produce fully Normalised Logical Data Models.

So what is Normalisation and why should we care about it?

In Normalised data models, the Attributes within each Entity are wholly dependent on the Entity instance.

If this condition is true, then the Entity is described as being Normalised. The technique that ensures all the Entities in our model are Normalised, is called Normalisation, as described in Key Point 46.

Key Point 46   *Normalisation is a technique that ensures the data values of the Attributes within each Entity are __wholly dependent__ on __only__ the Unique Identifier of the Entity.*

There are various levels of Normalisation and these are certainly worth investigating when you get time. However, in this book, we are going to concentrate on a degree of Normalisation called Third Normal Form.

When I first started data modelling, a colleague of mine came up with the following phrase to encapsulate Third Normal Form[37].

Key Point 47   *The Attributes of an Entity must depend upon the Key of the Entity, the whole Key and nothing but the Key.*

---

37 There are other levels of Normalisation but this is the one that most modellers refer to as Normalisation and most Normalised data models attempt to achieve.

This is great once you understand the principle, but what does it mean, and how do you get to Third Normal Form?

Let's try to see the basis of the technique from the perspective of the data modelling *process*.

So far we have discovered that *things* of interest for an organisation can be defined as Entities. Starting to add Attributes to the Entities in our data models, begins a process of providing rigour for their definitions.

It may seem quite obvious to say this, but the Attributes need to 'belong' to the Entity in which we define them. What we mean by 'belong' is that their values must be related purely to the Entity *instance*. This implies that their definition must have a dependency on the Unique Identifier of the Entity.

For the majority of the Attributes we define, we intuitively tend to add them to the correct Entity. For some of them though, as we start to probe their meaning, we notice that actually we have inadvertently added them to the wrong Entity!

As a result of these 'ill-fitting' Attributes, we are forced to recognise that we need to add new Entities and associated Relationships. This recognition is the trigger for us to carry out Normalisation.

Ultimately, the process of adding these new structures will ensure that we define a fully Normalised data model.

There are two ways that Attributes indicate an additional Entity is required. These are either the addition of a new;

1. Master Entity or

2. Detail Entity

Firstly we'll look at the creation of Master Entities.

Gaining A New Master Entity

In some 'ill-fitting' Attribute scenarios we are forced to the conclusion that we need to add new Master Entities.

To help us understand how this comes about, let's look again at the Unique Identifier example that we developed for our Organisation Entity in chapter 7.

To create the Unique Identifier, we needed to add an extra Attribute to combine with the Registration Number to ensure its uniqueness as illustrated in figure 43.

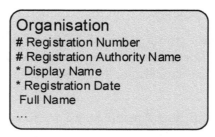

Figure 43 – Organisation repeating Attribute values

Let's remind ourselves of the sample data that could fill the structure of figure 43 in the following table.

Registration Number	Registration Authority Name	Short Name
123456	Companies House	Supernova Industries
456732	Companies House	FutureAnalytics Ltd
654321	Companys House	Retro Interiors Design
654321	Educational Institution	St Bartholomew Academy

Looking at this data, we immediately notice that the Registration Authority Name of 'Companies House' is being repeated. This *repetition* suggests that the Attribute contains data *describing an <u>instance</u> of another Entity*.

In other words, there is some 'thing' whose single instance definition *persists across potentially more than one instance* of the Organisation Entity. Therefore its value *cannot be wholly dependent on the Unique Identifier of this Entity*.

In the example of our Organisation's Registration Authority, this 'thing' should contain a single instance of the 'Companies House' value. Of course, the 'thing' is a missing Entity.

Immediately, we realise that this missing Entity has a One to Many Relationship with the Organisation Entity.

This structure is one that we recognise straight away as a Master Detail Relationship with our original Attribute needing to be part of the new Master Entity.

This is an example of where an Entity did not occur to us in our first-cut, it has come about because after more detailed analysis, we recognised that an Attribute demanded the creation of a new Master Entity.

This provides an example of the Normalisation technique and illustrates how it has come about.

This Normalisation transition pattern is illustrated schematically by figure 44.

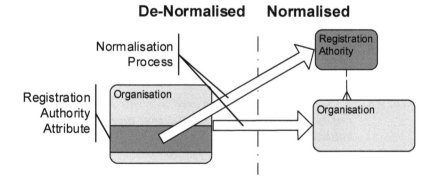

Figure 44 – Organisation Registration Authority

However, this example is really part of a standard resolution pattern that we need to add as a Tool to our Toolkit.

Generalised Master Entity pattern

What we have described in the previous section is an example of a generalised pattern in our data modelling, where *repeated values* in an Attribute suggest the creation of a Master Entity as illustrated in figure 45.

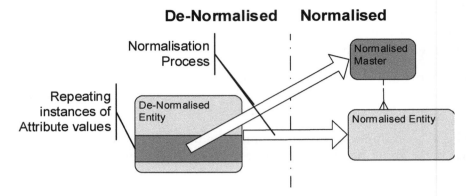

Figure 45 - Normalisation Tool producing Master Entity

Notice also that there was a clue to the existence of the Master Entity being required, because we started to qualify several Attributes with a name that indicated the existence of the Master Entity. In this case the prefix of 'Registration XXX' should have triggered some alarm bells and made us look carefully at why these Attributes all referred to some other 'thing'.

Key Point 48   *A strong indicator for the need to create a new Master Entity is one or more Attributes that contain <u>repeating values</u>.*

There are several beneficial consequences of Normalisation that are described in the following sections.

Removing redundant data

Let's look at a brief set of example data for our newly created Registration Authority Master Entity.

Registration Authority Data

Code	Name
COMPANIES HOUSE	Companies House
EDUCATIONAL INSTITUTION	Educational Institution

There is something that becomes apparent with our Normalisation example. Because we are taking the repeating data instances out of the Organisation

Entity and representing them once only in the new Master Entity, we are reducing data redundancy.

If we look at the 'Retro Interiors Design' Organisation instance in the table on page 102, we notice the misspelling of the Registration Authority Name as 'Companys House' instead of 'Companies House'.

Normalisation allows us to ensure the name is corrected by simply altering a *single occurrence* in the new Master Entity. This is because the repetition of the Name value of the Registration Authority is eliminated. In the absence of Normalisation, we would have had to correct every misspelling in the values of all of the instances in the Organisation Entity.

This provides a further benefit of Normalisation.

Initially we may have only noticed one or two Attributes that indicate this new Master Entity needed to be created. But what I have noticed repeatedly, is that as soon as it is created, you quickly begin to identify other Attributes that need to be recorded for it.

In the example of our Registration Authority, we realise that it may be good to record other Attributes such as its contact address and a web site URL.

Figure 46 – New Normalised Master Entity

Figure 46 illustrates the addition of other related Attributes to our newly created Master Entity.

Gaining A New Detail Entity

We have seen how one pattern of 'ill-fitting' Attributes drives the Normalisation process and results in new Master Entities. Let's now turn our attention to those Attributes that through Normalisation demand the creation of a new Detail Entity.

When thinking about the Organisation Entity we defined, there is a clue to the existence of a missing Detail Entity. This example comes about as a result of the decision to record the street address of the Organisation.

The following Attributes could be added to do this:

- Address Line 1

- Address Line 2

- City

- Post Code

- Country

Thinking about it a bit more though, which Organisation address does this represent? Is it the Registered Address or another one?

As soon as we ask this question, it becomes immediately apparent that actually more than one Address can be linked to a single Organisation, either concurrently or over time.

If we decide that we need to record a Registered Address *and* a Postal Address, are we going to add these as groups of Address Attributes as illustrated in figure 47?

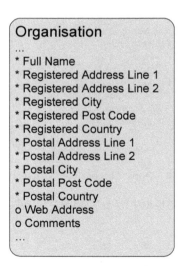

Organisation
...
* Full Name
* Registered Address Line 1
* Registered Address Line 2
* Registered City
* Registered Post Code
* Registered Country
* Postal Address Line 1
* Postal Address Line 2
* Postal City
* Postal Post Code
* Postal Country
o Web Address
o Comments
...

Figure 47 – Organisation repeated Attributes

Obviously we cannot keep on adding the repeated group of Address Attributes to the Organisation Entity.

However, let's just pause for a moment to analyse what is going on. Because *repeating groups* of the Address Attributes are being defined, we can tell that there could be *many instances* of this Attribute group related to *each instance* of our Organisation Entity.

Therefore, this repeated set of Attributes is not wholly dependent on the Entity Unique Identifier, since there could be many instances related to a single instance of the Entity. The repeating group of Attributes really describes a related Detail Entity.

It is quite clear that in the case of our Organisation, the new Normalised Detail Entity we need to create, is the Organisation Address.

With this model we are now able to add as many Addresses to the Organisation instance as are required. This can be achieved without needing to add new Address Attribute groups to the Organisation Entity.

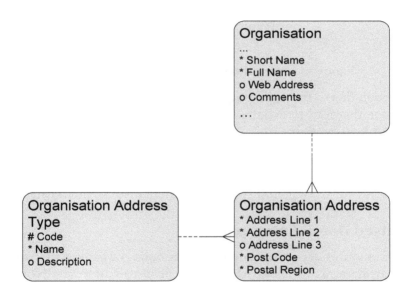

Figure 48 - Organisation Address Detail Entity

Notice in figure 48 we have added an Organisation Address Type Entity. This could contain the following example values:

Code	Name
REGISTERED	Registered
HEADQUARTER	Headquarter
POSTAL	Postal

What this model provides us with is a future-proofed or extensible model. This is because if new Types of Addresses are discovered we can simply add these new Type instances as data into the Address Type Entity. Importantly, we have not 'baked into' our data model the Address Types as we would do if we list them explicitly in the original Entity as groups of Attributes.

The pattern that leads to the creation of this Detail Entity through Normalisation is illustrated in figure 49.

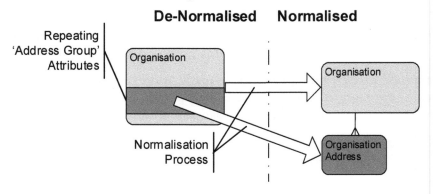

Figure 49 – Normalisation producing Detail Entity

Notice though that in the preceding example, there were already clues to help us determine the need to create a Detail Entity. The clues were the *repeating groups* of Address Attributes.

When we record these repeating sets in the Organisation Entity we find that we need to qualify them in some way in order to indicate in which of the repeating sets they belong; in this case, 'Registered XXX' and 'Postal XXX'.

Generalised Detail Entity pattern

The qualification of repeating individual Attributes, or groups of Attributes, immediately alerts us to check whether we need to add a new Normalised Detail Entity. This is because each repeating individual or repeating set of Attributes tells us that the Attributes values' *are not wholly depend on the Unique Identifier of the Entity.*

Key Point 49   **A _repeated single_ Attribute, or _repeating groups_ of Attributes indicate that Normalisation needs to take place, resulting in a new Detail Entity being created.**

But this Address resolution is a single example of a more generalised pattern illustrated in figure 50.

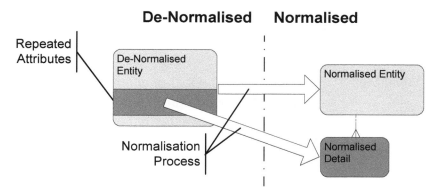

Figure 50 – Normalisation Tool producing Detail Entity

So the clues for creating a new Detail Entity are:

1. Repeated single Attribute or

2. Repeated groups of Attributes

Sneaky De-normalisation

Even experienced Data Modellers can produce data models that are highly Normalised, but actually contain sneaky De-normalisations.

We would never think of adding each Client Order as an additional Attribute into the Client Entity, but something very similar to this is often done with other kinds of Attributes!

One of the most common examples is where date Attributes start to be repeatedly added, to cover at least some of the Lifecycle dates of the Entity.

Only recently I came across a good example of this scenario. It became apparent that what had started out as a simple Attribute in the first few days of my data modelling, revealed that it was actually an example of a De-normalised Attribute.

How did this come about?

In the Business area I was modelling, Digital Marketing Campaigns are key high level Entities. Obviously each Marketing Campaign has many Attributes one of which is the Planned Start Date.

However, what became apparent almost immediately, is that in addition to tracking this date, the dates of other significant events associated with the Marketing Campaigns needed to be recorded, for example, Planned End Date and Initial Review Date.

We now recognise that the *qualified* repetition of these Attributes gives us a clear sign that a new Normalised Detail Entity needs to be created as illustrated in figure 51.

Figure 51 – Resolving sneaky De-normalisation

However, in many data models these kinds of Attributes are explicitly added into the Entity, in what we now know is a clear breach of Normalisation!

Clearly this new Detail Entity is an example of recording Lifecycles for our Entities which is a topic we will return to in chapter 14.

9: Relationships As Unique Identifiers

Introduction

Our Toolkit already contains the core Tools allowing us to create data models that define maps of our organisations' data landscape. We have also learned of the importance to be able to uniquely identify each instance of our Entities.

Attributes provide a Tool that is able to provide a Unique Identifier for many Entities. However, uniquely identifying every Entities' instances is one of the trickiest areas in data modelling. We have already seen that the Tool based upon Attributes alone, was not adequate in defining the Unique Identifier for every Entity.

In chapter 7 we used an example of identifying a Client's payment in response to their enquiry. It became apparent that this problem is made easier, if we are able to look for payments that relate to the Client.

Therefore we realise that in many cases, an Entity's Relationships will be crucial to uniquely identify it.

In this chapter, we will learn how to extend our Relationship Tool to form a part of an Entity's Unique Identifier.

Relationships As Unique Identifiers

In chapter 7 we saw that one or more Attributes can be used to define a Unique Identifier for an Entity.

Although this is a standard approach, there are many examples where it still does not allow us to fully differentiate between Entity instances. You will also come across Entities that cannot use Attributes to fully define their Unique Identifier because they don't have any! Admittedly these situations are rare, but you will definitely encounter them.

How then will you create a Unique Identifier for these scenarios?

We require a new Tool that can be used to ensure the uniqueness of an Entity's instances, and this Tool is the instance's Relationship to one and only one Master instance.

The often quoted example for this is the Order Items that appear on an Order.

Key Point 50   *A Mandatory Relationship to one and only one Master Entity instance can be used to __partially__ uniquely identify an Entity instance.*

In this chapter we'll examine how to use Relationships, called Identifying Relationships, as part of an Entity's Unique Identifier.

Key Point 51   *Relationships that are used as part of an Entity's Unique Identifier are known as Identifying Relationships.*

In Barker Notation they are represented using a cross bar as in figure 52.

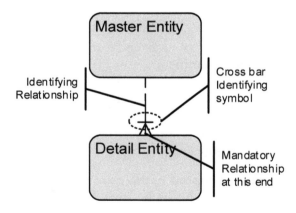

Figure 52 – 'Identifying Relationship' Syntax

This pattern provides one of the most powerful Tools in our modelling Toolkit! Without any doubt you will need this pattern repeatedly in your models, and a detailed description of its use is provided in the following sections.

Identifying Relationships as partial Unique Identifiers

The Identifying Relationship between a Detail Entity and its Master Entity can be used to *help* ensure uniqueness of the Detail instances. But the Detail

Entity instances *cannot be wholly* uniquely identified using a *single* Identifying Relationship.

If you think about it, if each Detail Entity instance is uniquely identified by being related to one and only one Master instance, this would describe a One to One Relationship. Effectively, this would make the Detail instance the same as the Master instance!

The fact that the Relationship Cardinality is a Many at the Detail Entity end, means that there could be *more than one Detail instance* associated with each Master instance.

If there can be multiple instances at the Detail Entity end for each Master Instance, then we still need to distinguish each one of them.

The only way for the Detail instances to be identifiable from each other is if there is something else in addition to the single Identifying Relationship that uniquely identifies them. In other words, we will need some other element to ensure their uniqueness.

Therefore in addition to an Identifying Relationship, a Detail Entity *must have as a minimum* either an additional:

A. Identifying Attribute or

B. Identifying Relationship

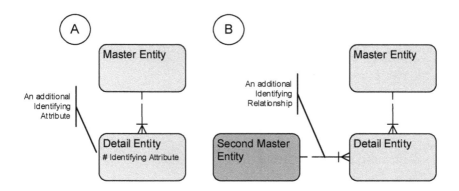

Figure 53 – Minimum Identifying Relationship requirements

Figure 53 illustrates the minimum combinations of elements required when using Identifying Relationships as Unique Identifiers for a Detail Entity.

> **Key Point 52** **When using an Identifying Relationship there must always be at <u>least one other component</u> of the Entity's Unique Identifier; either an Attribute or an additional Identifying Relationship.**

The following sections describe this fundamental rule more fully.

Additional Identifying Attribute

One option to complete the Unique Identifier of an Entity, is to add an Attribute to it in the Detail Entity.

Adding an Attribute to complete the Unique Identifier typically has two patterns:

1. Sequencing within Master

2. Non sequenced within Master

These are described in the following sections.

Additional Identifying Attribute - sequencing within Master

Where an Attribute is used in combination with an Identifying Relationships to define the Unique Identifier, it is possible to use a numeric Attribute which increments as the number of Detail instances increases. Often it starts with the value of 1 for the first instance and increments by 1 as well.

There are two patterns for this:

1. Surrogate Identifying Attribute

2. Natural Identifying Attribute

Let's look at these in a more detail.

Surrogate Key Attribute

It is possible to add a Surrogate Key Attribute to an Identifying Relationship, to create a fully formed Unique Identifier for a Detail Entity.

The example often cited for this scenario that is easy to understand is an Order and corresponding Order Items.

In this pattern, the Detail instances have a Line Number Attribute added to the Order Item Entity. In this example and many others, the Surrogate Key is defined to start at 1 *within* each Master Entity instance, for example, within each Order.

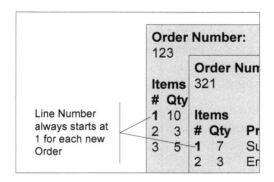

Figure 54 – Surrogate Attribute - Sequencing within Master

Notice that when using this option, the extra Attribute is *not Unique* across *all* the instances, *all* the Orders will have an Order Line instance with a Line Number of 1!

A fragment of this model is illustrated in figure 55.

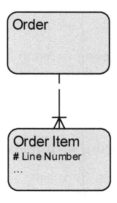

Figure 55 - Relationship as part of a Unique Identifier

In the model fragment shown in figure 55 we see that the Order Line Items are *partially* defined by being contained in a specific Order, but become totally uniquely identified by the combination of the:

1. Line Number[38] *and*

2. Identifying Relationship to one and only one Order

This seems to be a good pattern, but there is something that is not quite right about using a Surrogate Key as the additional Identifying Attribute in the first place.

If we think about it for a moment, the Line Number actually contravenes one of our fundamental principles as a Data Modeller, which is that the *meaning* of the data is everything.

If the meaning of the data is everything, then what is the meaning of a Line Number? Is it the sequence of the data capture? Is the sequencing of the Items important because there is some interdependence of them?

Generally, in fact, this example passes none of the tests as to whether the Attribute conveys any meaning at all. In truth, we use it as a convenience in the absence of any other way of differentiating the instances.

An alternative to consider might be the Date (including a time component) at which the Order Line Item was created. This at least has a real significance. When transforming the Logical Data Model into an implemented system, this Date Attribute could be converted into a more typical Line Number Attribute representation, should this be required.

But what are the alternatives?

One alternative is to consider using a second Identifying Relationship, which we'll explore a little bit later in this chapter. For the moment though, let's consider how it is possible to use a Sequencing within Master pattern *and* have the meaning that we consider essential in our data models.

Natural Attribute Sequencing within Master

The previous example used a Surrogate Key in combination with the Identifying Relationship to ensure uniqueness, but what about using a Natural Attribute? These scenarios are not that prevalent, but do occur.

---

38   There is something to notice here though that is not often mentioned; because the Line Number is a Surrogate Key, we could in fact simply make it *unique* across all the instances of Orders. This would mean that actually the Relationship need not be an Identifying Relationship at all! If we implemented any systems based upon this data model, it would be very easy for us to convert the Surrogate Key into a number that is 'Sequenced within Master' on any User interfaces including UIs and Reports.

When using a 'Sequencing within Master' pattern, the Data Modeller should examine the possibility of using Attributes that have a Real World significance and only resort to a Surrogate Key in the absence of a viable Real World Attribute.

An example that illustrates where an Attribute can be used in addition to the Identifying Relationship *and* does have Real World meaning, is illustrated in figure 56.

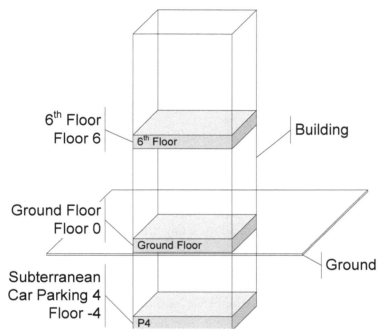

Figure 56 – Building Floors in the Real World

In figure 56, Building Floors exist within the context of a single Building and so are uniquely defined in the data model, by an Identifying Relationship to the Building.

We can use the Floor Number Attribute, in combination with the Identifying Relationship to a single Building, to create the Unique Identifier of the Building Floor.

This will provide a solution that the following example data illustrates:

Building Level sample data

Floor Number	Floor Name
-4	P4
0	Ground Floor
6	6th Floor

This satisfies the Unique Identifier requirements using a 'Sequence in Master' pattern. But unlike our Order Line example, the additional Unique Identifier Attribute has a meaning in the Real World.

The model fragment that illustrates this is in figure 57.

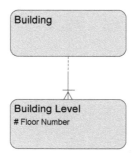

Figure 57 - Building Floors fully Uniquely Identified

Notice in this example that either Floor Name, or Floor Number could satisfy our need for an additional Attribute for our Unique Identifier[39].

However, you may wish to use the Floor Number[40] as this is unlikely to change over time, whereas the Floor Name may change for all sorts of different reasons and within relatively short timeframes.

This example is a good illustration of an Attribute that has Real World meaning being used in conjunction with an Identifying Relationship to create a Unique Identifier.

Additional Identifying Attribute – *not* sequencing within Master

In the preceding sections we have seen that a 'Sequencing within Master' Attribute can be used to ensure the Uniqueness of the Detail Entity.

---

39   Earlier in chapter 7 we mentioned that it is difficult to come across Natural Keys and Alternate Keys. This is an example where we have both!

40   In the Real World the Stacking Sequence Number is probably a better choice than even the Floor Number.

However, there are many instances where the Detail Entity *already* has one or more other Attributes that can act in combination with the Relationship to ensure Uniqueness. But these Attributes do not use the 'Sequencing within Master' pattern.

As an example of this let's return to our Organisation Entity. In chapter 7 we discovered that the Organisation can have a Unique Identifier Attribute that is Mastered by a Registration Authority, for example, its Company Registration Number.

But these numbers cannot be guaranteed to be unique, and could potentially clash with Registration Numbers that are governed by other Registration Authorities. In other words, a Registration Number can only be guaranteed to be unique within the context of a specific Registration Authority.

Thus, it is the combination of its Registration Number and the Identifying Relationship to a single Registration Authority that is guaranteed to be unique. We now have the visual syntax in our Toolkit to record this understanding in our model fragment as illustrated in figure 58.

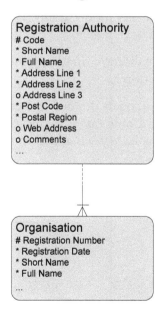

Figure 58 – Identifying Relationship and Attribute as Unique Identifier

So far we have covered three patterns where an additional Attribute has combined with the Identifying Relationship to form the Unique Identifier.

Additional Identifying Relationship

To explain how additional Identifying Relationships can be used as part of the Unique Identifier, we'll return to the simple Employment model fragment we saw in chapter 6.

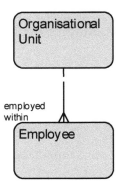

Figure 59 – Simple Employment model

But the Employee Entity in this model fragment is really a conflation of a Person and an Employment.

We'll rectify this using Normalisation by adding the Person Entity as a Master of a redefined *Employment* Entity.

The Employment Entity is uniquely defined by being associated with one and only one Person and one and only one Organisational Unit. The Identifying Relationships that define this have been added to the model in figure 60.

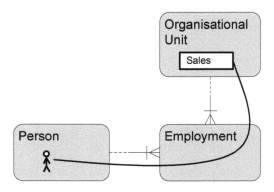

Figure 60 – More mature Employment model

But this is not quite the whole answer. An immediate question we should ask is raised by the temporal aspect of this model.

The question it raises is 'can a Person be employed by the same Organisation *more than once?*'

I think that for more than a single Employment to occur concurrently, the answer is likely to be no. However, over time we would definitely need to allow for this possibility.

The way this can be done is by using a combination of the techniques we have covered so far. We will need to use a combination of Identifying Attributes and multiple Identifying Relationships as described in the following sections.

More Complex Combinations Of Unique Identifiers

So far we have concentrated on the minimum requirements to create Unique Identifiers using Identifying Relationships.

Even using an additional Attribute or a second Identifying Relationship may not provide the uniqueness that we crave to define our Unique Identifiers.

The following sections describe more complex scenarios.

Many to Many Unique Identifier Relationships

In chapter 6 we created a standard resolution Tool for M:M Relationships, using an Intersection Entity as a pattern. This Tool provides a quick first-cut for your model that you can then assess and enhance as required.

Let's review this Tool in the light of our new knowledge of Identifying Relationships.

What wasn't included in the pattern at that point, was that the two new Relationships *must* form at least part of the Unique Identifier of the Intersection Entity. This is because they represent a *unique instance* of a Relationship between the two original Entity *instances*.

Therefore the standard resolution pattern can be modified to include the Identifying Relationships as in figure 61.

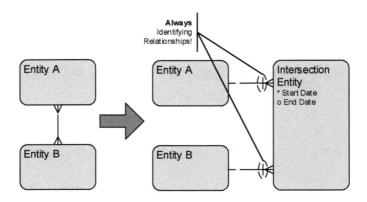

Figure 61 – Identifying Relationships for Intersection Entities

We can apply this Tool to the Employment model that we just looked at in figure 60 and confirm that apart from the Date Attributes it is equivalent.

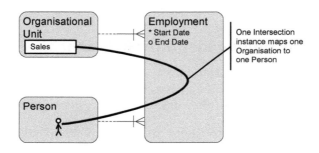

Figure 62 – Two Identifying Relationships pattern

The model illustrated in figure 62 allows an Organisation to employ one or more People, and each Person can be employed by one or more Organisations.

But a single Organisation can only be the employer of a one Person *once* – that is, for ever!

This cannot be correct. Let's examine this in a little more detail.

Recurring instances of Intersection Entities

Notice in figure 62 that our Tool has Attributes added to it that track the basic Lifecycle dates of the Intersection Entity as default[41].

---

41   In fact before considering their removal, you would need to question carefully why you *wouldn't* track these dates.

Whilst it is typical to add the date range for the life of the Intersection Entities, it is not *required* for the date Attribute to be a part of the Unique Identifier.

However, we must always ask 'can the Relationship represented by the Intersection Entity exist *more than once?*'

Imagine a Person employed by an Organisation, who leaves it and then returns a while later. It would not be enough to define the uniqueness of each of these Employments only using the Identifying Relationships. This is because as soon as the Person returned we would need to record another Employment instance between the same combination of the Organisation instance and the Person instance. This would violate its Unique Identifier.

Look at the example data[42] in the following table for an illustration of this.

Organisation	First Name	Last Name	Start Date
ABC Co.	Dave	Knifton	17/04/2016
ABC Co.	Dave	Knifton	09/08/2019

This clearly illustrates that in the absence of the Start Date, the repeating periods of employment between 'ABC Co.' and 'Dave Knifton' would violate the Unique Identifier. Therefore a better model is to add the Start Date Attribute into the Unique Identifier in addition to the two Relationships as in figure 63. Once this becomes part of the Unique Identifier there is no longer a violation of the Key caused by the Person's repeated employment.

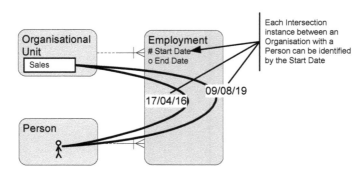

Figure 63 – Two Identifying Relationships plus Start Date pattern

The model in figure 63 allows there to be multiple Relationships recorded between the Organisation instance and the Person instance, as long as they have different Start Dates.

---

42   For the sake of clarity I have De-normalised the data in this table.

10: Advanced Relationship Modelling

Introduction

In terms of our Relationship Tools, we have already learned the basic syntax and techniques enabling us to define the structures in our models. We have also extended the power of these so that they can be used to form a part of the Unique Identifiers of our Entities.

But this is only the beginning of how Relationships can be used to fully define the data patterns in our data models.

In this chapter, we will use the same symbolic syntax that we are already familiar with, but consider some standard modelling patterns that you will undoubtedly need in your data models.

Also we will describe what happens when it is the same Entity at both ends of a Relationship. This is an extremely powerful Tool that you will use repeatedly in your models. Because of this, we will highlight some illegal patterns for its use and this will save you time from otherwise having to discover them for yourself.

Firstly though, we will consider a variation of the Many to Many Relationship pattern that we are familiar with called the Fan Trap. Although this pattern is often characterised as a problem, when used correctly, it can provide a very powerful Tool.

Fan Traps

A Fan Trap is the description given to a variation of the M:M Relationships where two Detail Entities are linked to the same Master Entity.

If ever mentioned, Fan Traps are almost always portrayed as a problem in data models. But this is not necessarily the case. In fact, if used correctly, they provide a powerful modelling technique.

Let's find out what a Fan Trap is to understand when it is an appropriate Tool, and when we would be wise to use a different pattern.

Figure 64 contrasts the two M:M Relationship resolutions.

The standard resolution Tool that we have seen so far involves the creation of a Detail Intersection Entity.

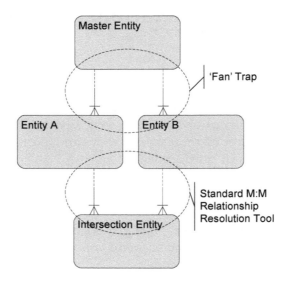

Figure 64 – Fan Trap compared with an Intersection Entity

The Fan Trap links two Entities via a common Master Entity. We can see however, that there is clearly still an M:M Relationship between the instances of Entity A and Entity B.

> **Key Point 53**   *A Fan Trap pattern is where the two Entities are linked via a shared Master Entity.*

To provide an example of the Fan Trap pattern, we will use a simple Entitlement model as in figure 65.

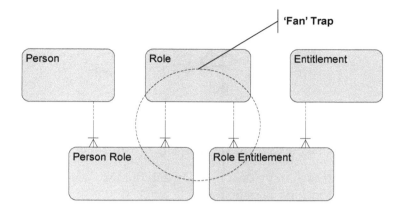

Figure 65 – Fan Trap example

What this model represents is that; each Person can have one or more Roles allocated to them and each Role can provide the authority for one or more Entitlements. Notice though, that the Role Entity is related to two Detail Entities and thus can be considered as the Master Entity in a Fan Trap.

> *Key Point 54*   *A Fan Trap pattern allows us to model the association of a set of data in one Entity with a second set of data contained in a second Entity.*

If we need to answer the question 'Which Entitlements does a specific Person have?' it can provide the answer, but the answer is a set of Entitlements. Equally, if we ask the question 'Which People have a specific Entitlement?' again the model can provide us with an answer, but the answer is a set.

Therefore we notice that this pattern provides a mapping of a set to a set.

It cannot provide a mapping of an individual instance in one set, to an individual instance in the other set.

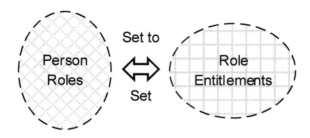

Figure 66 – The set mappings of Fan Traps

If we need to map each individual Relationship then we need to use an Entity to track the Relationships as in figure 67.

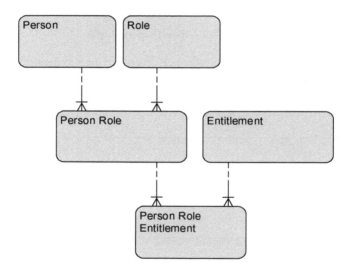

Figure 67 – Standard Intersection Entity example

Please note though that these two model fragments are definitely not equivalent to each other! The difference can be illustrated by considering the need to add a new Entitlement to a specific Role of 'Administrator'.

The Fan Trap model will allow us to add the additional Entitlement to the Role. The *set* of People who are currently allocated this Role, would immediately 'inherit' the new Entitlement.

In the model represented in figure 67, we would need to find all the People who have been allocated the Role and allocate the new Entitlement to each and every one of them *explicitly*.

But the second model does provide finer control over Entitlements, because we can explicitly add or remove Entitlement allocations *individually*.

So although the Fan Trap is almost universally portrayed as a problem in data models, this is not necessarily the case. It is a representation that needs to be validated, but if used appropriately, is actually a very powerful pattern to use and we'll add it into our Toolkit.

Recursive Relationships

We have learned that Relationships tie Entities together to form the structure of our data model. In the previous sections we have enhanced our understanding further and added the pattern of an Identifying Relationship as a Tool into our Toolkit.

In the following sections we'll consider a new pattern that will inevitably occur somewhere in almost all of your data models. This pattern is where the Relationship ties an Entity back onto itself and is called a Recursive Relationship.

This type of Relationship is normally is used to record a hierarchical structure of some kind within the data. Look at the model fragment in figure 68 which illustrates just this kind of data relationship.

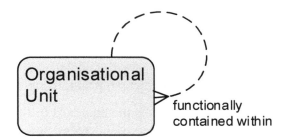

Figure 68 - Recursive Relationship Model

What the model fragment represents is that each Organisational Unit may be functionally contained within one and only one (Master) Organisational Unit.

The above model represents the Real World relationships shown schematically in figure 69.

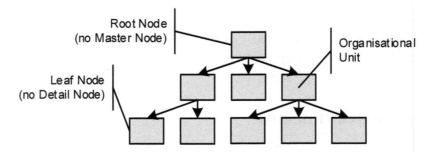

Figure 69 - Real World Recursive Relationship data representation

Notice in this structure that there are two special Node Types[43]:

1. Root Nodes – Nodes that have no Master Node

2. Leaf Nodes – Nodes that have no Detail Nodes

The following sections look at what these Recursive Relationships represent and how you can use them in your models.

Taxonomy

One of the key uses of Recursive Relationships in data models is to represent Taxonomies.

This term is used a lot in data realms. It refers to the way we like to categorise things. If we look at figure 69, we can clearly see that this categorisation capability is exactly what the Recursive Relationship allows us to record.

A good example of a Taxonomy is the Standard Industry Codes that you may need to incorporate into your models at some point. A small subset of the entire listings is listed below.

- M - Professional, scientific and technical activities
    - o   69 - Legal and accounting activities
        - ▪   691 - Legal activities
        - ▪   692 - Accounting, bookkeeping and auditing activities; tax consultancy
    - o   70 - Activities of head offices; management consultancy activities

---

43   Nodes represent Entity instances.

Bill of Materials

Another way to think about the Recursive Relationships is to think about them as representing a Bill of Materials structure (BOM).

The BOM term refers to the Engineering and Manufacturing terminology where a list of components is required to make up a larger component. This larger component in turn can be a part of another larger component.

As an example, think of a car door; this is a component part of a car, but is itself made up of other components. Many of these constituent components are themselves also made from other components parts.

Although common within Engineering and Manufacturing models, this pattern has far wider applicability than these fields. In fact it provides a powerful Tool that I am sure you will use many times during your modelling.

Illegal Recursive Relationships

Since Recursive Relationships provide such an important pattern, let's take a look at some rules about Recursive Relationships that you need to be aware of.

No Mandatory ends

Notice that both ends of the Relationship must be optional.

If you think about it, this has to be true.

If it were not optional at the Master Entity end, then the Hierarchy would have no Leaf Nodes, as each Leaf Node would need to be the Master instance of one or more Detail instances.

If it were mandatory at the Detail Entity end, then each Master instance would require its own Master instance!

Therefore there would be no ultimate root node.

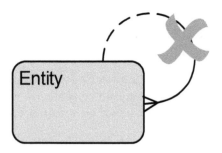

Figure 70 - Illegal Recursive Relationship

Key Point 55   *Both ends of a Recursive Relationship must be optional.*

This means that the model in figure 70 is an example of an invalid Recursive Relationships.

Illegal Recursive Relationship as Identifier

Recursive Relationships cannot be used within the Unique Identifier of the Entity.

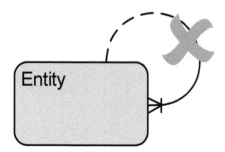

Figure 71 - Illegal Identifying Recursive Relationship

The Recursive Relationship model in figure 71 is illegal on two counts:

1. It would need to be mandatory in order to be a part of the Unique

Identifier[44]

2. As the levels progress the Unique Identifier would need to get bigger!

Key Point 56 *Recursive Relationships cannot form any part of a Unique Identifier.*

No One to One Recursive Relationships

As an extension to the rule that there should not be any One to One Relationships in your data models for Relationships, the argument is also applicable to Recursive Relationships.

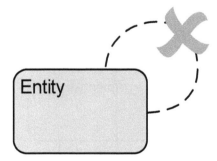

Figure 72 – One to One Recursive Relationship – cannot exist

Key Point 57 *Recursive One to One Relationships cannot exist.*

No Many to Many Recursive Relationships

Whilst not strictly speaking *illegal*, this is a variation on the M:M Relationships

---

44   Refer to the preceding section as to why this cannot be.

pattern. Therefore these need to be resolved within a Normalised Logical Data Model.

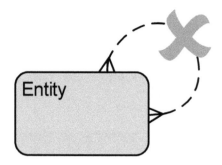

Figure 73 – M:M Recursive Relationship – needs resolution

This pattern can be seen as a specific instance of two Entities being related through an M:M Relationship. The only difference is that the Entities at each end of the Relationship are one and the same.

Therefore we can adapt our standard M:M Relationship resolution Tool to provide a standard pattern for its Recursive counterpart, as shown in figure 74.

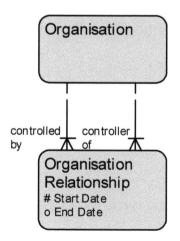

Figure 74 – Resolved M:M Recursive Relationship

> ***Key Point 58*** ***M:M Recursive Relationships must be resolved in***
> ***Logical Data Models and these have a standard***
> ***resolution pattern.***

What the model in figure 74 represents is the resolution of the M:M Relationship that:

1. each Organisation can be the controller of one or more other Organisations and

2. each Organisation can be controlled by one or more other Organisations

If, for the same combination of Master Entity instances, it is possible for a specific Organisation to Organisation Relationship to end and then be re-instated, a temporal component would need to be added.

To illustrate this in the example in figure 74, the Start Date of the Organisation Relationship has been added to the Unique Identifier.

Cyclical Recursive Relationships

Notice also that the patterns in the preceding Recursive Relationships do not prevent the Detail Instance from being the Master Instance of its Master Instance, at one or more levels above it in the hierarchy. Figure 75 illustrates such a network of instances.

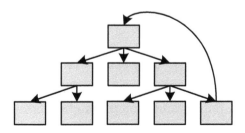

Figure 75 - Cyclical Recursive Relationships

This is a pattern that needs to be fully investigated if using Recursive Relationships in your data models.

Of course, in the Real World these kinds of scenarios actually do exist. As an example, if we think about the relationships between organisations, this may be a valid model of the Real World, even if only for those organisations that are up to no good!

Multiple Hierarchy Types

Obviously Hierarchies can have multiple Root Nodes. But there is a nuance to this where the Root Nodes and their Hierarchies can be of different Node Types.

This is shown schematically in figure 76.

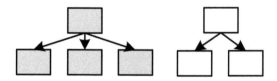

Figure 76 – Multiple Hierarchy Nodes with differing Node Types

The data model fragment to support this is illustrated in figure 77.

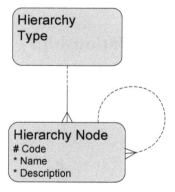

Figure 77 – Multiple Hierarchy Nodes with differing Node Types

We will revisit this model fragment again in chapter 13 where we will extend it by incorporating Rule Based Modelling techniques that introduce more rigour to the model.

Many to Many Recursive Relationships' Resolution Grouping Pattern

If we look at the model fragment in figure 74, this fits the idea of a hierarchy of the Entity instances. This is suggested by the Relationship names such as 'controller of' which indicate a 'direction'.

Other examples of these directional Relationship definitions include; 'owns' or 'contains'.

However, in the Real World there is not always a 'direction' for the way that the instances relate to one another.

As an example, if we think about the way that organisations can be commercially related. One option is the creation of Joint Venture vehicles that can be formed from multiple other legal entities. There is not necessarily any 'directional' pairings of Relationships here, and therefore the hierarchical concept doesn't necessarily hold true.

Key Point 59 *Some M:M Recursive Relationships may not have a direction and therefore may not represent a hierarchy.*

In these scenarios, every instance is implicitly *related* to every other instance in the group, as illustrated in figure 78.

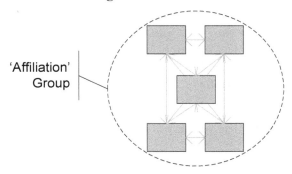

'Affiliation' Group

Figure 78 – Recursive Many to Many Grouping Entities

For these data patterns, the model in figure 74 is not appropriate. Instead the grouping model in figure 79 is a better representation.

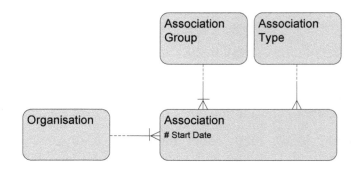

Figure 79 - Recursive M:M Relationship grouping model

You will need to probe the way that the Entities in the Many to Many Recursive Relationships are related to each other, to see whether there is any 'direction' before deciding on your resolution.

'Typing' Of Master Entities

If we return to our Organisation Entity for a moment, we realise that in common with many other Entities, the instances come in different 'flavours'.

Immediately upon creating a new Entity, we should consider adding an Attribute to indicate the 'flavour' of the Entity, which we would call the Type.

In chapter 8 we learned that this Attribute would need to be Normalised into a Master Entity because it will certainly have repeating values of the Type Attribute. Therefore we can see that for the majority of our Entities we will need to add Typing Master Entities.

Although I call these Entities '[Entity Name] Type', for the actual values that are recorded within them, I use the term 'Domain of values'.

The Typing Entities form a special class in your data models known as the Reference or Master Data[45] Entities. These are the ones that record the *context* and *meaning* for either, other Reference or Transactional Entities.

Although there can be Types of Types, this is less common and Types of Types of Types are rare in my experience.

---

45   If they are subject to some Master Data Management controls – which, of course, they should be!

The vast majority of Transactional Entities and even many Reference Entities are typified in this way. So a question that is possible for you to ask with every Entity you create would be; does it have one or more typifying Master Entities?'

In the example of Organisation, quite obviously not all Organisations are of the same Type. The Organisation Type is a critical part of our understanding of each instance of the Organisation Entity.

For example, we would think about and probably treat Companies differently from Charities. The latter may be offered discounted prices and there may also be specific Tax implications of dealing with them compared with Companies.

Let's add this new Organisation Type Entity as in figure 80.

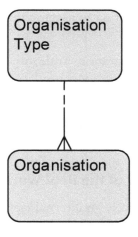

Figure 80 - Organisation Type

This all looks fine. However earlier, we said that each Organisation instance is defined by its Registration Number *and* its related mastering Registration Authority.

This Registration Authority is also a Master Entity and does seem to implicitly indicate the *kind* of Organisation we are recording, so which is the true Typing Entity for Organisation?

Multiple Typing of Entities

It is possible to have more than one Master Entity that defines the 'Type' of an Entity.

Where we have multiple candidate Typing Entities we need to be vigilant as to whether there is total, or any overlap between them in terms of their meaning.

For example, in the case of our Organisation Entity we have two Master Entities that are potentially the Typing Entities for it.

They are:

1. Organisation Type

2. Registration Authority

This raises the immediate question of whether the Registration Authority is the same 'thing' as the Organisation Type?

The answer is not as straightforward as it might seem at first sight. If there is only one Registration Authority per Organisation Type and these map one to one, then it might be tempting to assume that these two Entities represent the same actual 'thing'.

That is, we can use the Registration Authority *as* the Organisation Type and vice versa. This would almost certainly result in us jettisoning the Organisation Type Entity since the other has a Real World significance.

But the thing we need to probe here is the extent to which the two Entities actually represent the same thing.

Internally Defined View of the Real World

Organisation Type is effectively an internal view of the external world.

We are grouping Organisations into Types based upon our own evaluation of the *meaning* of their Type. The Types of this internal evaluation are subject to change over time and this is driven by internal forces.

Externally Defined View of the Real World

Registration Authorities are *real* things in the external world.

Their *meaning* is not defined purely by our internal view of them, but rather driven by external forces. As an example, these forces could cause the Registration Authorities to be replaced by one or more other Registration Authorities over time[46].

---

46   As a concrete example of authoritative bodies changing; in 1997 a Regulatory Body called the Financial Services Authority (FSA) was created from the previous Securities and Investments Board to regulate the UK Financial Services industry. In 2012 the FSA was replaced by the Financial Conduct Authority (FCA).

By applying this perspective to our judgement reveals that there is a definite fault line in the meanings of these two Entities, and one that will become more exposed over time.

A model we could define at this stage would therefore look like the one in figure 81.

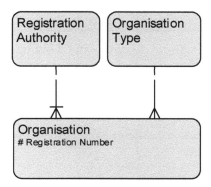

Figure 81 - Organisation Type and Registration Authority

If you are developing Global data models, the Registration Authorities will almost certainly be different within different jurisdictions across the world, which is an aspect we will consider in chapter 13.

By contrast, the organisation's definition of Organisation Types should be *conformed* across the globe and this, if nothing else, will determine that the two Entities are not the same.

The Unique Identifiers of 'Typing' Entities

It is worth spending a moment to discuss the Unique Identifiers for your Type Entities.

As mentioned earlier, these Entities typically define the organisation's internal understanding of its data. Whereas the other externally defined Entities, will (hopefully) come with ready-made Unique Identifiers, the Types typically do not.

This means that in the absence of any recognised Natural Key or externally Mastered Key, your organisation will be creating one. So let's look at our Registration Body and create some sample values for it.

Registration Body Entity Example Values

Code	Name
COMPANIES HOUSE	Companies House
EDUCATIONAL INSTITUTION	Educational Institution
HEALTH TRUST	Health Trust

Note that the Code Attribute forming the Unique Identifier is actually a Surrogate Key. Although the *instances* our Entity contains are all created in the external world, there is no *externally defined Domain* for them. We are defining the Domain internally and thus the definition of the *Entity* is totally under the control of the organisation. We decide what constitutes a Registration Authority. This is in distinct contrast to the Person Entity where the instances are also externally created.

I am a big fan of using an alphabetic code to uniquely identify each occurrence as I find these are:

1. easier to get ratification from operational Stakeholders and

2. provide easier and speedier resolution in forensic investigation of data quality issues in any implemented system

I also recognise that this datatype is not universally popular for Surrogate Keys and many Data Modellers adopt a numeric identifier instead. Their argument runs like this; if the Unique Identifier 'Code' values you used need to be changed, then you would have to update all the data that references the alphabetic Key throughout the implemented system landscape.

I could object to this implementation argument on the purist grounds that, at the Logical Data Model definition stage, we should not care about any potential implementation. But this argument may not be easy to win within your own particular organisation.

However, I can honestly say that I have *never* faced this challenge. Maybe by taking a little more time to fully qualify and define the Entities their Type definitions and values for the Domains, the number of times in my experience when the Unique Identifier Code needs to have been changed has been zero.

It really doesn't matter which way you go, but it is a good idea to use a consistent convention across all the data models that you produce.

Domain Value Ratification

Another consequence from the creation of Typing Domains is that of needing to define the values for these Domains. A key decision for you will be to decide how far you go with ratifying the values contained in the Domains with stakeholders.

Obviously some of the values contained in your Domains need to be defined, even if this is so you can feedback the meaning of the Domain with stakeholders.

However, to what extent do the values need to be ratified before you can be confident of the Domain's definition? If you do define them more fully in your data models, how would you keep the values synchronised going forward? If you don't keep them synchronised, then your examples may not resonate with key stakeholders, or will become stale very quickly and hence create confusion in the future.

This is an example where using a Data Lexicon can pay dividends.

Your data model can refer to this and because this is external and accessible, it will be easier to keep current if the Domains get modified over time.

It may be wise to create enough example values to:

- ensure that there are no higher level categories that act as Types of the Types

- convey a clear understanding of the Domain with stakeholders

You may be fortunate because there are defined processes already within your organisation that can carry out the more time consuming Domain ratification activities. If there are, then this will allow you to decouple your efforts from this otherwise extremely time consuming activity, and get on with the business of data modelling.

Data Typing Spectrum

Some of the data we want to record is Transactional and driven by Real World Events. However, it is the meaning framework that conveys the context for these and therefore provides the benefit to the organisation. This framework is largely constructed using Type Entities.

As we get into the detail of our data models, we start to define Typing Entities and as a result, we begin to understand something about the Entity that is defined at a more abstract level than the Entity instances themselves. But how far can we go with this Typing of Entities?

Decisions - Abstracting Domains

The abstracted Type Entities we create can themselves sometimes be further grouped or typified and also have their own extensive Attribution and Relationships with other Entities.

> **Key Point 60** *Abstraction provides a way of grouping definitions and meanings that exist at a level above the individual instances of data.*

We all know that the process of abstraction to higher levels can be carried out repeatedly, until all discernible meaning is ultimately lost from a data model.

Even at lower levels of abstraction, this important technique can provide a *barrier* to understanding.

The Data Modeller may need to consider how to mitigate the disadvantages arising from extensive Type abstraction in their modelling, whereby it sometimes results in the meaning of the model becoming obscured.

Transactional Versus Reference Data Entities

After creating data models for many organisations that have different operational processes, it becomes clear that one organisation's Transactional data could be viewed as another organisation's Reference Data.

As an example, for some organisations the creation of a Customer is almost always associated with each sale transaction. This makes their view of a Customer quasi-transactional.

For other organisations, their Client base is actually quite stable and therefore the list of Clients can be treated as Reference Data.

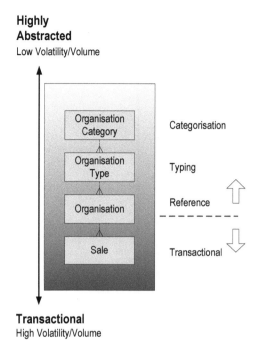

Figure 82 –Transaction Data and Reference Data spectrum

This gives rise to the idea that actually there is a spectrum from the highest data volatility data to the lowest data volatility as illustrated in figure 82.

Where we draw the line for the delineation of Reference Data on this spectrum is a little bit arbitrary, and will depend to a great extent on your organisation's operations.

11: Things that Are The Same But Different - Super-Type Modelling

Introduction

A recurring theme surrounding the definition of the Entities in our Logical Data Models is the way that *different* types of Real World things are thought of and treated operationally in very *similar* ways by organisations.

For example, People and Organisations can be treated almost identically by some Business areas in organisations. This leads to the idea that despite their obviously different physical manifestations, they can be viewed as being the same 'thing' in many operational respects.

This chapter describes the way that we need to think about the Entities that operationally have a lot in common and yet are not the same thing. To model the above scenario we'll introduce the technique of Entity Super-Typing as a modelling Tool.

Correctly grouping Super-types can be quite tricky and abstraction has got a role to play in getting this modelling technique right.

Sometimes things that should be grouped as the same thing are not, and at other times, things are grouped together that don't really belong together. This chapter will provide a simple check-list to help you assess whether your adoption of a Super-type Tool to group Entities is correct.

In chapter 6, we looked at an example where Relationships between a Detail Entity and two different Master Entities could be mutually exclusive. In this chapter, we'll look at how to formalise this rule using Arcs, and then compare it to the Super-type pattern.

What Are Super-type Entities?

People and Organisations are physically really very different in the Real World.

Yet they are both legal entities and as such can play very similar roles in the commercial and financial world.

Over the years I have developed many models for many kinds of organisations. A key theme that has kept recurring is that for many organisations, the way that People and Organisations are treated operationally has more similarities than differences.

Their differences in the Real World naturally give rise to differences in their Attribution and also the Business and Data Rules that surround their data capture within the organisation. But one thing we notice though, is that they have many parallel Relationships with other key Entities in our models. At some point you cannot help but be aware of the parallels in all aspects of the way they are treated, *apart* from their physical manifestation.

This is where the concept of Super-types originates.

We should consider using Super-types whenever Entities conceptually represent the *same thing*, but their Real World manifestations are distinctly different.

Key Point 61   *Super-types conceptually represent the same 'thing' for an organisation's operations, but exist as different things in the Real World.*

Super-type Check List

So how can you check whether the adoption of the Super-type pattern for two or more Entities is valid?

The following check list can be used to verify whether the pattern is appropriate.

Challenge
Are the Sub-types represented by different physical manifestations in the Real World? (Could one of them be defined as any of the others over time?)
Are the Sub-types all treated in similar ways by our organisation?
Is there a small and stable set of these Sub-types?
Are the Sub-types' Relationships with other Entities similar to each other?

If the answer to any of the questions above is 'No', then this should make you stop and re-evaluate whether the use of a Super-type is valid for the data model you are defining.

To help clarify the use of Super-types let's look at another example of a Super-type drawn from within the Telecommunications industry. The example we'll use is where signal transmission can be performed by very different physical media including:

- Metallic conductors
- Fibre optic cables
- Radio wave Radiation
- Microwave Radiation

Although these are physically very different in the Real World, they can all be thought of as Signal Media for the data transmission parts of a Telecommunication Network. Because of their functional and operational similarity, they are ideal candidates for Super-Typing.

Super-type Syntax

In Barker notation the Sub-type Entities are shown as being *contained* within the Super-type. Note that this is not the same as overlapping.

So for example, the model to represent the Signal Media as above, is shown in figure 83.

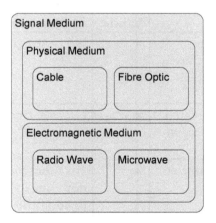

Figure 83 - Super-type Entity example[47]

To my mind this notation is very elegant and has a simple intuitive feel about it.

The notation indicates that an instance of a Sub-type can never be represented as an instance of a different Sub-type. This is true both concurrently and over a period of time. This should *never* be an issue though, because of our rule about them needing to be very different things in the Real World.

---

47 Notice that the levels of nesting can be one deep only, or indeed higher than just the two levels shown here.

Invalid Super-types

Where Super-Typing is less successful, is where the Real World manifestations are actually very similar, but the way that the organisation interacts with the Sub-types is different.

I often see material that uses examples similar to figure 84 as a Super-type, when in fact it passes none of the tests for Super-typing.

Figure 84 – Classic, but invalid, Super-type example

Let's see how this example stacks up against our check list.

Check	Valid?	Explanation
Are the Sub-types represented by physically different manifestations in the Real World?	✗	No - they are all People.
Are the Sub-types all treated in similar ways by our organisation?	✗	No - we treat our Clients nicely. ☺
Is there a small and stable set of these Sub-types?	✗	No - these are the ones for now, but soon we will need to add others.
Are the Sub-types' Relationships with other Entities similar to each other?	✗	No - Clients are on the demand side whereas the Employees are typically on the fulfilment side of the data model. This means that their Relationships will be very different in the model.

After running through the check list we can see why this Super-type is not a good representation of the Person Entity. Because the Client and Employee are represented in the Real World by similar things, but the way the organisation treats them is different, we need to adopt a different modelling approach. In the next chapter we will learn how to model this scenario using a pattern of Roles.

Orthogonal Sub-types

If we ignore the challenge of the Sub-types being physically different, we leave ourselves open to the problem of the Sub-types potentially being orthogonal. So what do we mean by this?

To make this clear let's look at the example of the breakdown for People engaged within an organisation. Although we may have chosen to have Sub-types of Full Time and Part Time, another way of Sub-Typing the Entities could have been along gender lines.

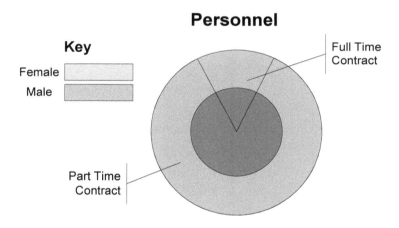

Figure 85 – Orthogonal Sub-type example

Because these Sub Types are of the *same* physical manifestation we can see that there are potentially lots of different ways that the same Entity instances can be grouped into Sub-types.

This makes the selection of only one of these possible ways somewhat arbitrary.

Straight away this gives us a strong signal that actually this is not a valid Super-type candidate. Of course, we only face this problem because we have ignored the basic tenet that the Sub-types must not be physically represented by the same thing in the Real World.

Attributes Within Super/Sub-type Models

We need to consider the positioning of Attributes in our Super-type models and what the impact of their location is.

If we place an Attribute in the Super-type then it is implicitly an Attribute of *all* of the Sub-types.

> **Key Point 62**   ___All___ *the Attributes of the Super-types are also implicitly Attributes of ___all___ of the Sub-types.*

Each of the Sub-types can have its own specific Attributes that are not shared by *any* of the other Sub-types nor the Super-type.

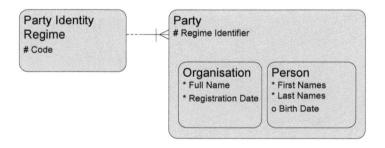

Figure 86 – Super-type and Sub-type Attributes

> **Key Point 63**   *Any Unique Identifier Attributes must be held in the Super-type.*

Relationships Within Super/Sub-type Models

We also need to consider the way that the Relationships can be attached to the Entities involved in a Super-type.

Key Point 64   ***All of the Relationships of the Super-type are implicitly to <u>all</u> of the Sub-type Entities.***

So if we look at figure 87, the Relationship between a Party and one or more Party Accounts is implicitly inherited by either an Organisation or a Person. This means that the Relationship can be described from the Order end as:

1. Each Party Account can be legally owned by one and only one Organisation **or**

2. Each Party Account can be legally owned one and only one Person

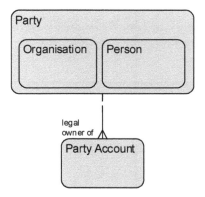

Figure 87 – Relationships of the Super-type

Key Point 65   ***Each of the Sub-types can have their own explicit Relationships that are not shared by either the Super-type, or any of the other Sub-types.***

In figure 88 we see that an Organisational Unit can only be a functional area of an Organisation and not the other Sub-type of Person.

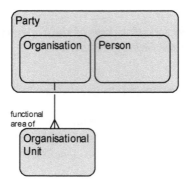

Figure 88 – Relationships of Sub-types

Key Point 66   ***Sub-types can have Relationships with other Sub-types and also Recursive Relationships.***

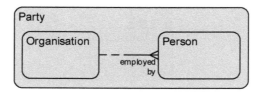

Figure 89 – Relationships between Sub-types

Figure 89 illustrates that a Person Sub-type must be employed by an Organisation Sub-type.

Key Point 67   ***Sub-types can also have Recursive Relationships with the Super-type.***

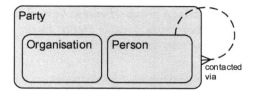

Figure 90 – Recursive Relationships from Sub-types to Super-types

In figure 90 the Relationship from the Person Sub-type to the Party Super-type indicates that each Party (Person or Organisation) can be contacted via one and only one Person.

Reading the Relationship the other way indicates that each Person may be the contact for one or more Parties (People *or* Organisations).

Unique Identifiers for Super-types

Combining all of the preceding patterns and the Unique Identifier patterns from chapter 9, we create the following definition concerning the Unique Identifier for Super-types.

> *Key Point 68* *Any Unique Identifier Attributes must be held in the Super-type and any Identifying Relationships must also be attached to the Super-type.*

Arcs

Arcs have a lot in common with Super-types and so in this section we will describe what they are, how to model them and how they compare with Super-types.

Arcs indicate that two or more Master Detail Relationships can be grouped from a single Detail Entity to multiple different Master Entities.

This grouping dictates that only one of the Relationships in the Arc can be true for each instance of the Detail Entity.

Key Point 69 ***An Arc defines a group of mutually exclusive Relationships from a single Detail Entity to multiple Master Entities.***

Earlier we described a scenario where each Employee can be employed by either:

1. an external Organisation, in which case we want to record the Organisation that employs them **or**

2. our own Organisation, in which case we will record which Organisation Unit they are employed within

We must record one of these Relationships but not both.

To do this in Barker Notation we can create an Arc as shown in figure 91[48].

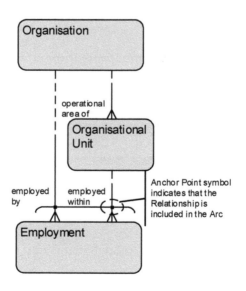

Figure 91 – Relationships in Arcs

Notice that the Relationships that are *included* in the Arc are marked with a dot.

This allows the Arc to span Relationships that do not participate in it. These would not have a dot where the Arc crosses the Relationship.

---

48   It is worth comparing figure 91 with the one we saw earlier in figure 32.

Because the Relationships attached to the Employment Entity are mandatory, what the model in figure 91 shows is an Arc that means each Employment *must* be:

- Employed by one and only one Organisation **or**

- Employed within one and only one Organisational Unit

We can see in figure 91 that the Relationships show clear parallels, albeit to different Master Entities. Earlier we mentioned that where clearly parallel Relationships exist this gives us a clue to represent Entities as Sub-types. So is there any equivalence between these two modelling styles?

Equivalency of Arcs and Super-type patterns

There is an overlap between the modelling pattern of Arc Relationships and Super-type patterns.

If we look at figure 92, we can see that the two models are actually equivalent in terms of the Relationships between the Entities.

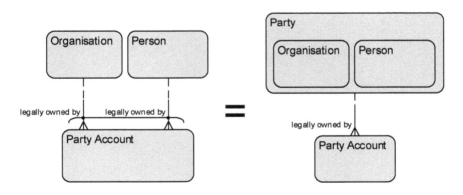

Figure 92 – Equivalent Arc and Sub-type models

Either model can be read as:

1. Each Party Account must be legally owned by one and only one Organisation *or*

2. Each Party Account must be legally owned by one and only one Person

One significant difference between the models is that the shared Attributes would need to be recorded in each of the Entities within the Arc model. In contrast, these would be recorded as Attributes contained in the Super-type

Entity in the other model.

So which one should you adopt?

To decide which way to model the above scenario, I would always use the principle that the model should be as clear as possible. If one representation leads to less clutter and/or structures that are easier to understand, then I would choose it as the best representation.

I would certainly not pay too much heed to any Physical design implications, since both modelling styles can be physically represented in the same way. Appendix C provides a description of the options for the way that the Super-type model for Person and Organisation can be implemented physically.

Of course not all data modelling tools support both of these representations and so the decision may be made for you because of the constraints of the modelling tool!

12: Actors' Roles

Introduction

In chapter 6 we discovered a powerful Tool that provides a standard pattern for the resolution of M:M Relationships. This involves the creation of an Intersection Entity that records the instances of the Relationships that exist between the two Entities.

In many models around the globe these Intersection Entities have a significance beyond a simple resolution pattern; what they actually represent are specialised Relationships.

In this chapter we will describe this concept more fully and describe typical patterns that we can add as Tools into our Toolkit.

Many of these specialised Relationships are to do with the Actors in our data models. Actors are those Entities that trigger or respond to the operational activities of our organisations, and thus create and modify the data represented in our data models.

The two most common Entities that have such an involvement are of course, Person and Organisation. These have figured in a lot of our examples so far, and so we will be able to revisit model fragments and apply a new understanding to them.

The way that we have looked at them to this point, has been to assume that *they* are the Actors.

In fact, in most cases the Person or Organisation possess capabilities and authorities that allow them to cause changes in our data landscape. But these powers form the basis of Roles which they are able to carry out.

It is actually through the Roles that the activities are executed, and therefore it is only in the context of these that they are truly able to become Actors in our data landscape.

Entity Roles

The journey we have taken so far has emphasised that there are two Entities that almost all of our organisations need to record something about and these Entities are Person and Organisation.

It is these two that typically have a direct impact on many areas in our data models because they drive the activities that cause data to be created or changed within our organisations.

When we communicate with each other about People and Organisations, it is easy to consider that it is the Entity instances themselves that are the Actors. As a result of this we intuitively want to connect all the Relationships directly to them.

In fact this is generally not the way that their Relationships should be modelled.

The ability of these two Entities to perform activities that create and respond to operational events, often needs to have special authorisation and possibly even regulatory, financial or legislative compliance. For instance a Buyer for an organisation will be acting on behalf of it, and is implicitly, or explicitly authorised to create debt on its behalf, in return for products and services.

For these specialised capabilities we typically use the term Role.

The Relationships to Entities affected by our Actors should therefore be attached to these Role Entities.

A major advantage of this Role model is that we cannot attach the Relationship to any Actor without them already having an appropriate Role. So unless a Person is already recorded as a Buyer for an Organisation, we cannot choose them to be associated with an Order.

Because of the constraints associated with the execution of the Roles' activities, their definition is often associated with many Business and Data Rules.

Key Point 70   *Roles represent the embodiment of capabilities, often requiring specific authorisation, or regime compliance to become the Actors in our organisation's data landscape.*

When we think about People having Roles, we notice that this is often under the auspices of one or more Organisations.

In chapter 6, we introduced the Relationship Tool and we looked at the idea that two Entities can have more than one Relationship between them. The example used illustrates two common Relationship types between our two key Entities that we are typically interested about:

1. On behalf of which Organisation are People are acting?

2. Who do we need to contact to liaise with a specific Organisation?

These Relationships between the two Entities can be represented by two explicit M:M Relationships as illustrated in figure 93.

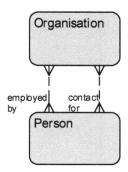

Figure 93 – Explicit Relationships

These Relationships actually represent specific Roles and the next sections describe two approaches to modelling these.

Explicit Roles

Using our M:M Relationship resolution Tool, we can create two Intersection Entities as resolutions to the model fragment in figure 93. Each one is *explicitly* created for *each* of the original M:M Relationships.

This would seem to be the obvious approach, and has the major advantage of retaining the meaning of the original M:M Relationships in the resolved model.

Figure 94 illustrates this approach.

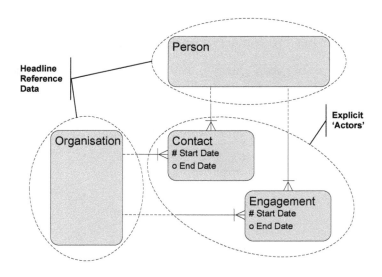

Figure 94 – Explicit Specialised Person Roles as Actors [49]

Whilst this seems to be the obvious modelling option, there is another as described in the next section.

Generalised Roles

An alternative to the preceding explicit resolution, is to model the multiple M:M Relationship Intersection Entities as a single generalised Intersection Entity as depicted in figure 95.

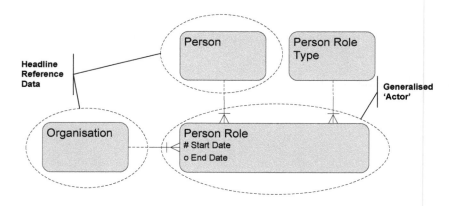

Figure 95 – Generalised Person Role as an Actor

---

49   The Contact Type and Engagement Type Entities have been omitted from this fragment for the sake of clarity and space.

Where this approach pays big dividends is made clear if we think about an example of representing the People involved in a Legal Agreement.

Each of these can be associated because they are carrying out specialist activities that they have a designated *capability to perform*.

For example the Person Roles could include:

- Vendor

- Purchaser

- Broker

- Solicitor

We do not attach the Relationships directly to the Person Entity. Instead we are interested in recording the *capacity* in which they carried out their involvement. Hence we attach the Relationships to the Person Role instead as illustrated in figure 96.

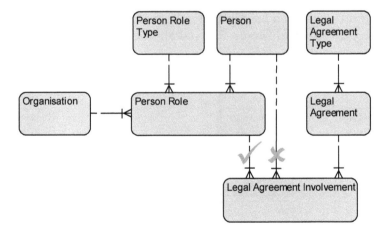

Figure 96 – Generalised Person Role

Here we clearly see the advantage of having a single generalised Person Role, since we can attach the Legal Agreement Involvement Entity to this *single* Entity. By contrast, if we used the explicit Roles approach, we would need to have many Relationships from the Legal Agreement Involvement Entity. One would be required for *each* of the explicit Roles, for example; Broker, Vendor and Purchaser.

So given the choice in your model, which approach is 'correct'?

Explicit Versus Generalised Roles

We have seen two approaches to modelling Roles; an explicit approach and a generalised approach.

There are consequences associated with whichever way you go.

If you do model Roles explicitly, one problem you will face is that it becomes more difficult to obtain a consolidated picture of them, for example, to produce a list of *all* the Roles played by any given Organisation.

What we have gained with the generalised resolution is an extensible and future-proof model for People as Actors within the context of Organisations. This approach also provides a simplified set of Relationships in our models because, for example, all of the Relationships related to Organisations as Actors are attached to the single Organisation Role Entity. In addition we don't have to revisit our data models every time we encounter a new Organisation Role Type.

But what we lose is the explicit understanding that was conveyed by the original model. This is an example of where abstracting the data structures causes it to be more difficult for stakeholders to understand them, as described in chapter 2.

So which is the correct model? The dilemma is illustrated in figure 97.

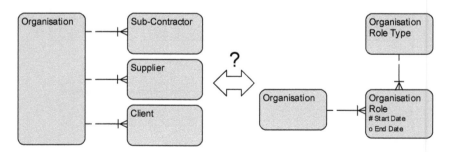

Figure 97 – Explicit versus Generalised Role modelling

As was already mentioned; a constant stream of decisions needs to be made during the modelling process and this is a good example of one such decision.

Either of the approaches is 'correct' is the honest answer, but you will need to decide which one to adopt based upon the constraints that you face at the time.

To help you make this decision here are some guidelines. If the answer to all of the following questions is 'Yes', then an explicit model may be more appropriate, otherwise the use of a generalised model may be the better option.

Question	Considerations
Is the set of Roles stable?	That is, no more new Roles can be envisaged and even if new ones do occur, they are introduced over timeframes measured in years.
Are the Attributes of each Role quite specific to each Role Type?	Typically Start and End Dates are important and then possibly a few others. In many data models most of the richer set of Attributes will probably be held in the Reference Data Entity, for example, Person.
Are the Relationships for each Role Type different and applicable to large areas of the model?	In the case of the Legal Agreement in figure 96 the Relationships are localised. However, there will be models where the Roles' Relationships apply to many other Entities across the entire model scope.

It may be that actually you adopt a mixture of the two approaches, using an explicit approach for a limited number of Roles. These are created because their Attributes, Relationships, Data and Business Rules differ widely from the others. In addition you can model the remaining more generally applicable Roles using a generalised pattern.

Common Explicit Roles

There are a number of commonly encountered specialised Roles that you will almost certainly come across. We have already introduced some of these, but whilst we are considering Roles, we will examine them in more detail.

The ones covered here are:

- Contact

- Engagement

- Client

- Supplier

These are described in the following sections.

Contact Role

In chapter 4 we looked at the importance of getting the names of things correct. The example of Person, Contact and Employee was used. In some data models there is no clear distinction between these Entities.

A Contact is often assumed to be interchangeable with Person, but a Contact is not a Person and a Person is not a Contact.

A Contact is a specialised Role that a Person can perform. You may wish to model this Role explicitly since it has:

- Attributes that are not necessarily shared by other Person Roles such as its contact details

- a number of Relationships that specifically apply to Contacts

Figure 98 illustrates a data structure that can record the Contact Preferences for Contacts. This is an example of why it makes sense to have an explicit Role for them, since these Relationship will not be shared by the majority of other Roles that People perform.

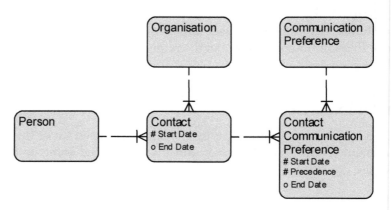

Figure 98 – Explicit Contact Role model

Engagement Role

The way that an organisation considers either internal or external Employees may be so markedly different from other Person Roles that it makes sense to make this an explicit Role Type.

In chapter 9 we saw this model fragment as illustrated in figure 99.

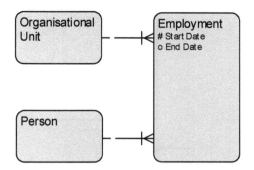

Figure 99 – Two Identifying Relationships pattern

So far on our journey this model has been progressed to the point where the Unique Identifier constraints are satisfied. However, I am sure like me, you feel some unease about the naming of the Intersection Entity as 'Employment' to describe the way that a Person and Organisation can be contractually bound.

You may want to consider using a more abstracted Role Type of 'Engagement' which, for example, could encompass:

- Permanent Contract

- Short Term Contract

- Fixed Term Contract

- Secondment

- Internship

Let's enhance this into a more general pattern by abstracting the Employment to an Engagement and adding an Engagement Type to control the Domain of values that are relevant.

A more flexible, but nonetheless explicit, Engagement Role would be as illustrated in figure 100.

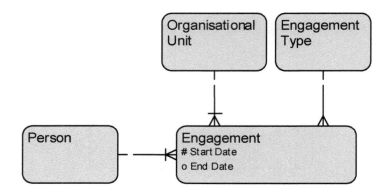

Figure 100 – Organisation and Engagement model

Notice here that the Unique Identifier includes the:

1. Relationship to Person

2. Relationship to Organisational Unit and

3. Engagement Start Date Attribute

This allows us to record multiple Engagements for a Person with the same Organisational Unit over time. But, it would not allow two Engagements between a Person and an Organisational Unit with the same Start Date, even if they are of different Engagement Types.

Supplier Role

Suppliers are another example of specialised Actors and therefore it may make sense to create them as specialised explicit Roles. This would allow their Relationships to other Entities to be more clearly modelled.

Suppliers are typically Organisations, but Organisations may also play other Roles in your data landscape, so it makes sense to model the Role explicitly related to an Organisation as in figure 101.

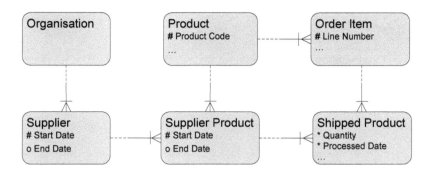

Figure 101 – Simple Supplier model

We have extended the model to include the Products that they are able to supply. We modelled the Contact Role explicitly because of its specialised Attributes and Relationships and, in a similar way, it makes sense to have an explicit model for the Supplier Role.

Client Roles

When we think of Client within the scope of our organisation, this may be restricted to:

- Individuals only

- Organisations only

- be either Individuals or Organisations

Typically, a Client is a specialised Role that any legal entity can play.

Earlier we looked at the idea of Super-types and this is a good way of representing the legal entities that can play a Client Role.

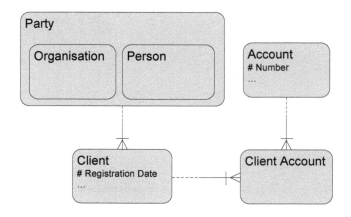

Figure 102 – Simple Client model

Notice that initially we may have wanted to relate the Client Account directly to the Party Entity but we have learned in this chapter that this is not a good approach. Not all Parties that we record would necessarily be Clients, for example, some could be Suppliers.

In addition, for a Party to become a Client, they may have to clear hurdles such as credit checks or financial and legislative regulations. Therefore the two 'things' are not the same and we need an Entity for each.

Client versus Customer

In chapter 2 the importance of defining Entity names correctly was emphasised. Typically the Entity names Client and Customer are used interchangeably. However, you may want to consider that there is a subtle difference to the names as follows:

- Client ⇨ Reference Data - because stable set of repeating consumers

- Customer ⇨ Transaction Data - because typically non repeating consumers

You may want to make the distinction in your naming of the Entity Role that is a consumer of your Products or Services

Customer implies a degree of anonymity, but interestingly Big Data has transformed our ability to recognise the repeating patterns of transactional data. Analysis of these patterns allows us to identify instances of the otherwise anonymous Customers.

Modelling Roles As Sub-types

Just before we leave Role definitions, I often see Roles modelled as Sub-types and wanted to just spend a moment considering this technique.

Role Types *can* be modelled *explicitly* as Sub-types of a Super-type Entity as in figure 103.

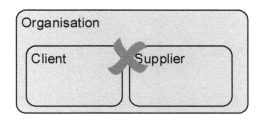

Figure 103 - Organisation Role as Sub-types

However, there are several reasons why this should be avoided, including:

- The occurrences of the Roles would need to be physically different things in the Real World - in which case they cannot be Roles of the same thing, in this case Organisation

- It is a conflation of the Entity definitions – an Entity and its Roles are cannot be the same thing

- It is not Future-proof – new Role Types would require explicit new data structures and if the model is implemented, potentially development effort

13: Rule Based Modelling

Introduction

I remember very well the day when a Development DBA came over to my desk and exclaimed 'We're not having any of that "Typey Type Type" stuff in *my* Database!' Having delivered his declaration of prohibition, he spun on his heel and stomped off back to his workstation.

One of the most rewarding experiences for me in my data modelling career, was to witness the total transformation of this individual, as he started to appreciate the power of abstracting and using Reference and Meta Data structures as:

1. defence against developers and

2. defence against dirty data and

3. providing rigorous development frameworks

After some months of us working together, he started to champion the approach and soon started to chastise those guilty of not modelling *correctly*; that is, of *not* using a "Typey Type Type" technique!

So what is "Typey Type Type" modelling? Why can there be hostility to it and what benefits can make it worth considering?

We know that the process of abstraction to higher levels can be carried out to create a framework of meaning. What isn't always appreciated is the ability to use these structures to enshrine Data and Business Rules in the data model.

Several benefits are described in this chapter including the ability to constrain data and also provide powerful extensibility and future-proofing capability into your models.

Rule Based Modelling Technique

Earlier we discovered that through the process of abstraction, the definitions and *understanding* of data patterns become defined in the Reference Data or Meta Data structures of data models.

The core concept of Rule Based Modelling is that these data structures can be used to define *rules* about the data's patterns. This is what the Development DBA described as "Typey Type Type" modelling.

Key Point 71   *Rule Based Modelling is an approach that formally uses the "Typey Type Type" concept to constrain patterns of data using abstracted data structures.*

At its very simplest, we can think about this technique being used to ensure that transactions are constrained by Reference Data Domains. However, we can extend this idea to create far more sophisticated structures that specify data rules and even complex behavioural aspects of the data.

Before we get into such degrees of complexity, let's take a look at a very simple example to make the technique clear.

Simple Rule Base Modelling example

Let's return to the conundrum of Organisation Type and Registration Authority. We'll assume that after some deliberation, we decided that the Organisation Type is related to, *but not synonymous with*, the Registration Authority.

If we review the Organisation, Organisation Type and Registration Authority model developed earlier, we had got it to the stage illustrated in figure 104.

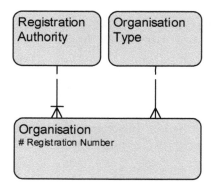

Figure 104 - Organisation Type and Registration Authority

This model looks fine at first glance; an Organisation instance is Uniquely Identified by a Registration Number allocated by a related Registration Authority. It is also defined as being of a specific Organisation Type.

The problem with this model is that there is a Real World correlation for the kinds of Organisation Types that each Registration Authority can allocate Registration Numbers. For example, Companies House in the UK cannot register Health Care Trusts. But if we read the model again, we notice that this is not constrained by the model definition.

But by changing the model slightly, we can use its data structures to record the *valid* combinations of Organisation Types that each Registration Authority can register.

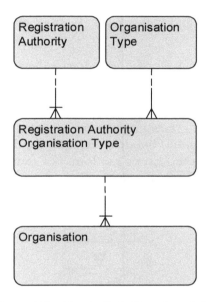

Figure 105 - Simple Rule Based model

The intervening 'Registration Authority Organisation Type' Entity will only contain valid combinations of Registration Authorities and Organisation Types. Thus it *will* include all the valid combinations such as 'Companies House' and 'Incorporated Company'. But it *will not* contain the combination of 'Companies House' and 'Health Care Trusts'.

Since an Organisation can only be related to one of the *valid* combinations, we have built a *data driven rule set* into the data model.

Notice something important about this simple change that is described by Key Point 72.

> *Key Point 72* **Rule Based data structures hold rules about data patterns that otherwise would need to be defined in either the codebase, or using some other mechanism!**

So now we have understood the basis for Rule Based Modelling, let us look at some further examples that illustrate the use of this powerful Tool.

Constraining Hierarchy Structures

We saw in chapter 10 how Recursive M:M Relationships can be resolved using our standard pattern. This Tool is excellent at modelling Taxonomies and BOM style hierarchies and will typically be used somewhere in the majority of your models.

Let's review it now in the light of our understanding of Rule Based Modelling.

In the examples we have seen so far, there have been no control structures to ensure that the hierarchical data actually makes any *sense*. This means that they do not contain any *Hierarchy structure definitions* to constrain the Types of Nodes within any given Hierarchy. As a result, the Node Types and their relationships to each other can be random. For example there is no defence against the scenario illustrated in figure 106.

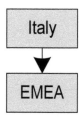

Figure 106 – Unconstrained Hierarchy model

In this scenario the 'Italy' Node is the Master Node of 'EMEA'!

What we need to add to our data models are Rule Based Modelling structures that will allow us to constrain the 'Country' Node Types to be contained within the 'Global Region' Node Types.

In figure 76 we saw that each Recursive Hierarchy can have multiple Root Nodes. This is a typical pattern where multiple Hierarchy Types can co-exist within the same structures.

Typically in this pattern, some of the Node instances can exist in several Hierarchies concurrently.

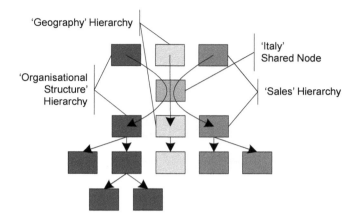

Figure 107 – Shared Node Hierarchy

Figure 107, illustrates where the 'Italy' Node exists in three Hierarchies concurrently:

- Geographical Region

- Organisational Structure

- Sales Region

To support this requirement means that our data model needs to provide a Hierarchy structure that allows a single Node to have multiple Master Nodes as well as multiple Detail Nodes.

The Rule Based structures that support these data requirements is illustrated in figure 108.

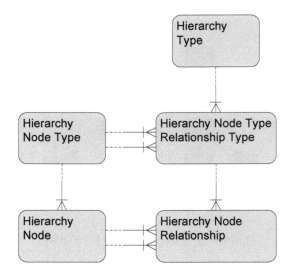

Figure 108 – Rule Based Hierarchy model

To understand how this additional structure has helped, let's see some sample data as in the tables below.

Hierarchy Node Type Entity

Name	Description
Global Region	One of the three Regions that the World market is divided into.
Sales Region	A large Sales Area encompassing several adjacent Countries.
Country	A country

Hierarchy Node Type Relationship Type Entity

Hierarchy Type	Master Hierarchy Node Type	Detail Hierarchy Node Type
Geography	Global Region	Country
Sales	Sales Region	Country

Hierarchy Node Entity

Hierarchy Node Type	Name
Global Region	EMEA
Sales Region	Southern Europe
Country	Italy

We can see that the rules contained in the Hierarchy Node Type Relationship Type Entity constrain that the 'Country' 'Italy' Node can have Master Node of 'EMEA' in the 'Geography' Hierarchy and 'Southern Europe' in the 'Sales' Hierarchy.

This is illustrated in figure 109.

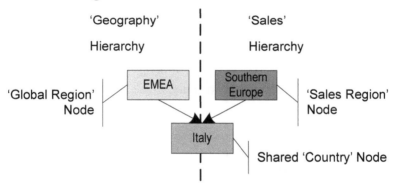

Figure 109 –Rule Based Shared-Node Hierarchy model

Reflection in Rule Based models

If we look at the model fragment in figure 108, we notice one of the most important principles that arises from Rule Based Modelling – that of Reflection.

This principle is based upon the premise that; if there are data rules about Entity Relationships at a specific level, then shouldn't these be reflected at the level of abstraction above or below it?

If we look at the model fragment in figure 110, we notice that there are two possible planes for reflection, the vertical and the horizontal.

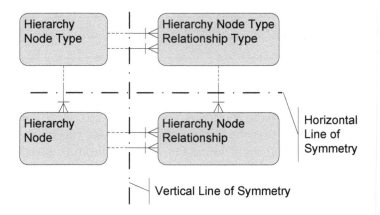

Figure 110 – Reflection in Rule Based models

These lines of reflection allow us to create a related set of Meta Data structures very quickly. And when we come to verify Rule Based Model structures we can use this principle of reflection to rapidly Quality Assure the structures.

> *Key Point 73*   *Reflection is a principle arising from Rule Based Modelling that indicates if structures are present at a certain abstraction level in data models, then it is highly probable they will exist at a level above and/or below it.*

Always remember though that any structures that are inferred by Reflection will still require due diligence to ensure that that they are valid.

Attribute Extensibility

Extensibility in the context of an organisation's data landscape, refers to the ability to accommodate new data patterns without significant effort or expense.

The expensive and slow part of many system developments and maintenance is the development effort. However, you can add a lot of value for your organisation by incorporating extensibility patterns into its data models.

Even though such implementation considerations should not *drive* your model, we need to be clear about exactly what level of Attribution to record in our data models.

Data Modellers should ensure that the Entities and data structures recorded in their data models are an accurate representation of the data patterns and ideally should have longevity baked into them.
What will vary over time is the data that these data models contain. Any __data__ changes will need to be made over much shorter timeframes. As a result the __data model structures__ will need to have future-proofing features built into them.

We have already described the benefits from using abstraction to ensure longevity, but there are modelling techniques that you can use to make any systems developed from your models much more data driven.

The benefit of doing this is for implementations is that the systems can use Reference Data and Meta Data changes to extend or modify their functionality, instead of requiring developers to make extensive changes to the codebase.

The system related savings and step changes in organisational agility can be dramatic.

The benefit is wider than this though. What it means is that the data models also have longevity defined into them. We said that car manufacturers' data models created 50 years ago should be immune to the manufacturing and technological advances made since then. This can only be true if the data captured could have adapted over the decades, and such pattern changes could be accommodated by the data structures.

In chapter 12, we looked at creating generalised Roles and by giving these a Type. By doing this we are able to make the Entities extensible, that is, we can add new Role Types into the data structure as required.

In this section we'll look at applying that same principle to the Attributes contained in Entities.

We'll use a Task Entity as an example to demonstrate the technique.

The problem with recording the detail about Tasks is that, although we know some of the headline Attributes for the Task and some of its Relationships, the more detailed data we will need to record will depend on the Task Type.

Yet when we are creating our data model definitions, we will simply not know the Task Types that will be required in the future. If we don't know the Task Types, then we can't possibly predict what detailed data would need to be recorded for each of them. Therefore, how can we add Attributes into our data model that will accommodate the Attributes for these *future* unknown Task Types?

In other words, we need to define a data model that will be as accurate and relevant in ten years' time as it is today. This means that the *structures will remain unchanged*, but the *meaning* of the data will be *controlled through data changes*.

> **Key Point 74**   *Future-proofed Data Models have structures that remain unchanged, but allow the data they contain to be changed, in order to define any new data patterns required.*

Notice that this is not the same as allowing the Users of a system to enter any data that occurs to them at the time! Our models must still introduce rigour and enforce data patterns and meaning, but in a way that can adapt over time. These changes will be as a result of controlled changes in the Meta Data contained in the Rule Based Modelling structures.

The simple model fragment in figure 111 illustrates the starting point for our extensible model. In terms of a concrete structure, this represents what is knowable at the time the data model is created.

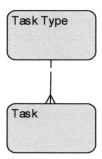

Figure 111 – Simple Task model

The next step is to add structures that can contain rules and hence be adapted to accommodate future definitions for Task Types, their associated Tasks, and the flexible Attributes required for each of these.

We'll start by adding a Task Attribute Entity. Figure 112 illustrates just such a structure.

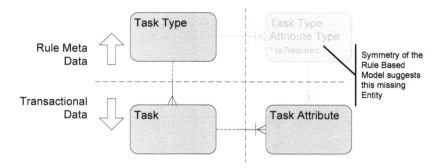

Figure 112 – Extensible Task Attribute model

Using our Reflection Tool from the preceding section, we can draw lines of symmetry into our model. As a result, we notice that there is an Entity implied but not yet present in our model.

By adding this 'missing' Entity of 'Task Type Attribute Type', we are now able to define the Attribute Types that are associated with any specific Task Type. When we get to the transactional world we will be able to capture data for any given Task Type using the Attributes of its appropriate Attribute Types.

The data in the following tables provides some samples for us to visualise how the structure in figure 112 would work.

Task Type Entity

Name	Description
Change light bulb	The replacement of one or more faulty light bulbs.
Add shelving to wall	The fitting of shelving to a wall.

Task Type Attribute Type Entity

Task Type Name	Name	Datatype	Description
Change a light bulb	Elapsed Time Number	Number	The time taken to complete the Task.
Change a light bulb	Elapsed Time Unit	Character	The Unit of Measure for the time taken.
Add shelving to wall	Elapsed Time Number	Number	The time taken to complete the Task.

Looking at the data in the preceding table, I hope you notice that the 'Elapsed Time Number' Attribute Type is being repeated. The Normalisation Tool that we acquired earlier allows us to correct the model for the missing element as shown in figure 113.

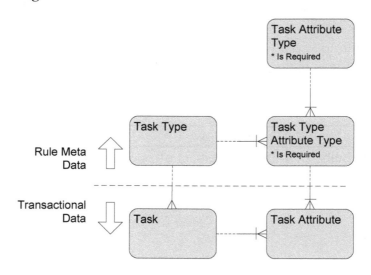

Figure 113 – Extensible Rule Based Modelling example

Now we can create a definition of each of the Attribute Types and re-use these in any specific Task Type Attribute Type that makes use of this definition.

Task Attribute Type

Name	Datatype	Description	Is Required?
Elapsed Time Quantity	Number	The number of time units taken to complete the Task.	Y
Elapsed Time Unit	Character	The Unit of Measure for the time units. For example; Minutes, Hours, Days.	Y

Notice that for a specific Task Type, the usage of a Task Attribute Type can be indicated as being Mandatory. This concept of providing defaults at a higher level that can be overridden at a more specific level, is a powerful feature that can be built into many of your Rule Based models.

Extensible Attribute Domains

In the preceding example we see that there is implicitly a Domain of values for the 'Elapsed Time Unit' Task Attribute Type. To model this relies upon the addition of a standard pattern as illustrated in figure 114.

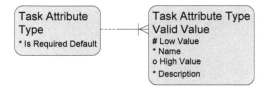

Figure 114 – Extensible Attribute Domains

This model supports the individual values such as 'Minutes', 'Hours' and 'Days'. It also supports ranges, for example 'A'->'E' using the Low Value and High Value Attributes. Note though that it also supports the combination of *both* within the *same* Domain.

Using the Rule Based Modelling Reflection Tool we can create a parallel structure at the Task Type Attribute Type level to override these 'default' values. Also we can add other Attributes, for example, Datatype, Format Mask and Display Sequence to enhance this capability further.

Globalisation and Localisation

When developing Global data models for any organisation there are common aspects to consider. Key though is the conformance of Global data definitions and the support of Local data definitions.

Typically in my experience, organisations want to conform their Global definitions whilst still maximising support of *all* of the Localised data requirements! As Data Modellers this gives us quite a challenge. Straddling these conflicting requirements for our data models is not the most comfortable position to be in.

One of the most serious challenges arises from the fact that you simply are not going to be able to consult with every business line in every part of the globe in which your organisation operates before you develop your model to the 'Good enough to go'[50] level of maturity.

The good thing is that actually a lot of what needs to be modelled is common across the globe. This means that you can get input from a limited number of 'reliable' sources from across the world to allow you to create the first-cut of your Global structures and Attribution. You can make any changes that are required, as and when input from other sources is possible.

We cannot cover every aspect of Global data modelling in this book, but we will highlight some common elements to include as standard patterns into our Toolkit.

These are:

1. Currency

2. Language

3. Regional Typing Entities

4. Attribution – Global versus Local

Let's look at these in more detail in the following sections.

Currency

Currency is the easiest of the major aspects to think about. To master the Currencies themselves is easy. They are relatively stable and I would suggest adopting the ISO Currencies for your Domain.

The only fly in the ointment here is the advent of the Bitcoin. But in a way the emergence of this illustrates how stable the Currencies are. The list of Currencies hardly ever fluctuates, the last major changes being the dawn and subsequent expansion of the Euro-zone. This has resulted in the individual

---

50   See the section on page 222 for more detail of this.

member countries' Currencies being removed from circulation.

There are also plenty of readily available sources for the mastering of the currencies' exchange rates in the Real World. This means that if your models ever need to be implemented, the decision about sources and frequency is relatively easy to satisfy.

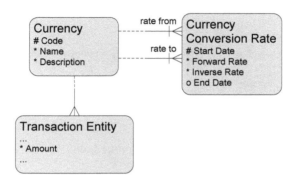

Figure 115 – Simple Currency model

Figure 115 provides a simple model fragment to illustrate the impact of Currency on your models. You will need to add a Relationship to the Currency Entity wherever financial amounts are being recorded in Entities within your data model.

Language

When developing Global data models, you may need to record Reference Data or Master Data in different languages.

There are a few variations for how to model this in your data models, one of which is illustrated in figure 116.

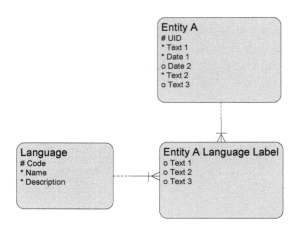

Figure 116 – Simple Language Label model

Rather than using a software tool to provide a pure translation or transliteration, this model fragment allows a more nuanced translation to be recorded. The structures will allow SMEs to record in different Languages, the *meaning* of Reference Data that is more operationally relevant.

Although this model is well suited to Reference or Master Data, it is not so good where Transactional data needs to be represented in different Languages in near real-time.

For Transactional data, a solution that relies upon a translation tool will be a better approach. If this is the case, then you may wish to create a placeholder structure in your Logical Data Model so that it is 'complete' but not spend time on getting into too much detail.

Notice that the Attributes of the Language Label Entity are *all optional*. This is because we cannot enforce that Mandatory Attributes in the Master Entity will have a Language equivalent defined.

If implementing this model, Views based upon the structures could use the Language Label values where these exist, and otherwise display the core Language values, for example, English. This is another aspect illustrating the ability for Rule Based structures to create overrides and defaults for data.

The model in figure 116 can be extended by creating an Intersection Entity representing the Locale which would be used to record the valid combinations of Language and Country.

This would support the requirement to have a different Language variation, for example, for the variations on the French Language that exist in France, Belgium and Canada.

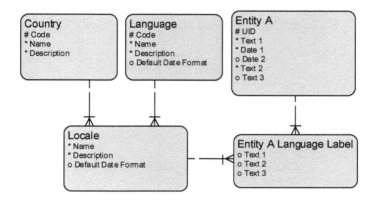

Figure 117 –Locale Label model

Notice that this model allows us to specify a Default Date Format. For example, this could be 'dd/mm/yyyy' for UK English, but could be 'mm/dd/yyyy' for US English.

Regional typing Entities

The Typing of Entities may require different values to be captured within different parts of the Globe.

If we return to the example of the Registration Authority we looked at earlier, we may need to add an Entity that will allow us to record the jurisdiction of the Registration Authority. To support this, we can add an Entity that will allow us to represent the various parts of the Globe, for example, Country. We can then use this to act as the Master Typing Entity for our Typing Entities.

For our Registration Authority, the model fragment in figure 118 will allow us to record the Country within which each body has jurisdiction.

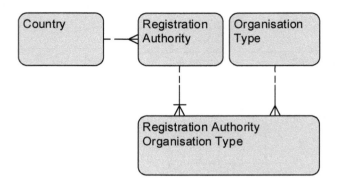

Figure 118 – Country Jurisdiction model

This looks good, but what about where the jurisdiction is across several Countries such as in the European Union. Here we would need a slightly more flexible structure for the way we can define each Geographical Region.

This Entity can contain Country definitions but also Supra-National areas. This will also work well for more Federal 'Countries' such as the USA, Germany and Australia.

It also copes with anomalies such as in the UK where England and Wales are often separated from the other 'Nations' of the Country[51].

For an example of Supra-National authorities, we can use Medical Bodies. These tend to have additional jurisdiction scope, other than purely Country level.

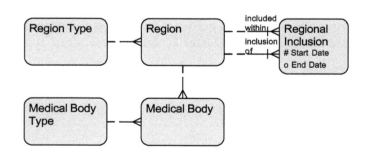

Figure 119 – Regional Area Jurisdiction

The model in figure 119 allows us to capture data as below.

---

51 These are Scotland and Northern Ireland.

Region Type	Region	Medical Body Type	Medical Body
Country	United Kingdom	Medical Association	British Medical Association
Nation	Scotland	Medical Association	British Medical Association Scotland
Region	European Union	Medical Research Body	International Board for Medical Research and Studies
Country	United States	Medical Association	American Medical Association

Notice the addition of Start Date and End Date Attributes in figure 119. These support the ability to record the dates when Regions can become included within, and then be removed from, enclosing Regions. A good example of this requirement is exemplified by the UK joining the EU and then Brexiting.

Attribution - Global versus Local

One of the biggest problems in defining models that cover the Globe is that of Attribute proliferation. This is caused by the need to add more and more Attributes as the model develops and as you get input from each Region and Country.

The proliferation of Attributes is obviously not a practical approach and leads to a lot of difficulty in the definition of the Attributes as well. For example, an Attribute that is Mandatory for an Entity in one Country, can have no significance in another and as a result would need to be made Optional.

This example makes it clear that as a data model incorporates Rules from more Countries, the data model will eventually offer little to assist with enforcing the Data and Business Rules.

The way to approach this is to use concretely defined data model structures for the Globally applicable Entities and Attributes. For the Regional and Locally applicable Attributes, the model needs to define Rule Based structures that will provide support for them through Meta Data definitions.

These can be seen as the Regional and Local extensions to the Global model. The pattern for this is illustrated in figure 120.

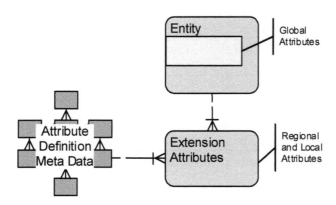

Figure 120 –Global, Regional and Local Attribute modelling

In the earlier section on Attribute Extensibility we considered the need to make the data model future-proof. The needs for Global and Regional data models can make use of the same Tool even though they are driven by different requirement.

Therefore in figure 120, refer back to the section on Attribute Extensibility to understand more about the Attribute Definition Meta Data.

14: Representing Lifecycles In Data Models

Introduction

The data that organisations need to record is primarily driven by events. As the events trigger responses and activities within the organisation, we can imagine that they leave vapour trails of data in their wake.

A lot of our data models are constructed to capture these vapour trails so that we can understand and report on what happened.

Some events are over very quickly, for example, a cash withdrawal from a bank cash machine is over in a matter of seconds.

For many other events the Transactional Entity has a lifetime during which multiple key events can be associated with it. If we just consider the online purchase of products for a moment; the selection of products and the financial payment events are over fairly quickly.

But these are simply the triggers for a chain of events. Part of this chain will be the logistics to ensure that the products are delivered to the Customer. But even when the products have been delivered, this may not signal the end of events associated with the original transaction, as further activities may occur, such as; replacing the goods due to faults, or repairing them under a guarantee.

What these examples illustrate is that many of the data models we create will have Entities whose Lifecycles are protracted and often vitally important for our organisations to track.

There is another major factor that has a significant impact on our data models and that is the ticking of time. As time moves on, certain instances of some Entities will be brought to life, others will be changed and yet others will expire. Our models need to have these temporal dependencies accurately represented as well.

Earlier in chapter 8 we saw that sneaky De-normalisation often arises as a consequence of needing to record Lifecycle and temporal aspects in a model. In this chapter we will look at the patterns required to take these into account and thus avoid sneaky De-normalisation.

Effective Date Pattern

The relentless passage of time will have a continuous and potentially dramatic effect on the data that your organisation relies upon. As the clock ticks, certain instances of some Entities will become current, some will be changed in some way, whilst other data will become no longer significant except from a historical perspective.

One of the simplest Tools to model Lifecycles and temporal changes, is to record the period during which the Entity instance is 'current', 'active' or 'effective'.

This is commonly called Effective Date processing. Typical names for the standard Effective Date Attributes are:

1. Start Date, End Date

2. Effective From Date, Effective To Date

Key Point 75   *Effective Date processing allows us to record the interval over which the Entity instance is considered to be; 'current', 'effective', 'active' or 'in-flight'.*

Figure 121 illustrates this concept schematically.

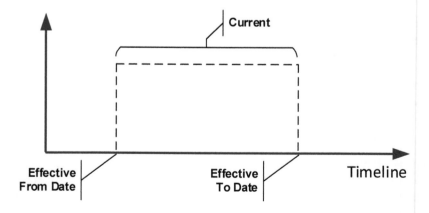

Figure 121 – Effective Date pattern

Where these Effective Date Attributes have special significance then this should be conveyed in their names for example:

- Acceptance Date

- Inception Date

- Termination Date

Effective Dates in Many to Many Relationships

One of the Tools we added into our Toolkit early in the book was the standard pattern used to resolve M:M Relationships. Almost without thinking, we can add the Effective Date Attributes for these, as in the vast majority of cases recording when the Relationship came into being and was finally deprecated will be important.

For most of our Explicit and Generic Roles we also need to include the date when these take effect and also the date when they are no longer applicable. Thus Effective Date Attributes are appropriate for these too.

Future-dating applicability

For some Entities we need to record Effective Dates that are at some point in the future at the time when we record them. For example, a Loan Repayment Schedule or a planned Project Start Date are recorded to take place in the future. These are simply a variation on our Effective Date pattern, and therefore can be based upon the same use of Effective Date Attributes.

So in figure 100 on page 168, the Engagement's Start Date can be set in the future as can the End Date if it is a Fixed Term Engagement.

Planned versus Actual dates

Often we are interested in when events are *planned* to occur, compared with when they *actually* occur.

This can be tracked by including Planned Date and Actual Date Attributes. For example:

- Attainment Planned Date, Attainment Achieved Date

- Payment Scheduled Date, Payment Received Date

Effective Dates in Reference Data

Reference Data also needs to use Effective Date Attributes to control the period for which a definition is current. So for example in our Organisation Type Entity.

Organisation Type Entity

Name	Effective From Date	Effective To Date
Charitable Trust	01/01/2005	
Limited Liability Partnership	01/01/2005	
Public Corporation	01/01/2005	17/03/2016

We can see that the Organisation Type of 'Public Corporation' has been deprecated as at '17/03/2016'.

States

The Effective Date processing pattern gives us a binary State during which the Entity is effective or current along a timeline[52]. For many Entities though this is not what is required, instead it is actually the Entity State that is important.

State is sometimes thought of as recording a progression through a Lifecycle but more often than not, this is truly the Status or Milestone that the Entity has attained.

A State should really represent a discrete data condition, for example, a simple 'On' or 'Off'.

But where it is possible for the values to recur, it needs to be Normalised into a separate Entity rather than being an Attribute of the original Entity.

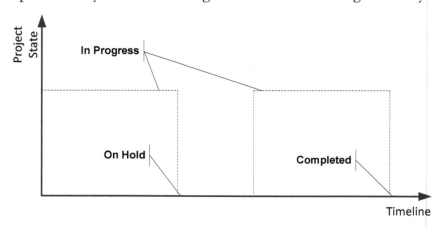

Figure 122 – Project State Lifecycle[53]

---

52 See figure 121.

53 Notice that even though the Project State is 'On' or 'Off' these can have nuanced meanings that require additional States to be defined as in this figure.

The data model fragment to support this State Lifecycle is illustrated in figure 123.

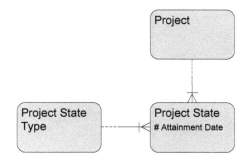

Figure 123 – Project State Lifecycle model

Notice here that there is no end date in the Project State. This is because the next Project State Attainment Date value will signal the end of the preceding Project State. In chapter 5 we learned that Attributes must have no dependency and if we added an end date Attribute this *would* have a dependency on the next Project State Attainment Date.

Status Transition Pattern

Status is very different from State as it implies a progression.

In the previous chapter we looked at how Rule Based Modelling can allow us to define data structures that can control behavioural aspects of data. This use of Rule Based Modelling techniques forms the heart of a Status Transition structure. This Meta Data structure is used to control the way that the Status of an Entity can progress.

As an example, imagine that we need to represent a simple Workflow for Clients to be able to request a new Account online.

Figure 124 illustrates the transition of the Status of the Workflow.

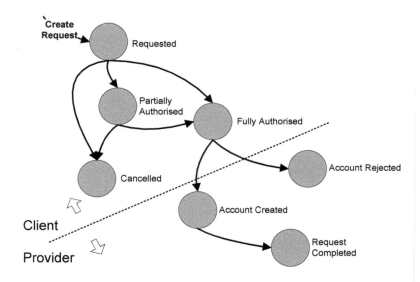

Figure 124 – 'Account Creation' Workflow status transition

In this example, the Client makes an online request to create the new Account and thus initiates a Workflow. The Workflow has various stages where other people from the Client organisation are able to take the Request through its authorisation stages. Eventually these may progress the request to a Fully Authorised Status, at which point the Workflow transfers to the Provider operational team. They carry out due diligence processes and, all being well, create the Account.

Notice how figure 124 actually depicts a Hierarchy. This means that we can re-use our Hierarchy pattern to form the basis of our Status Transition pattern as illustrated in figure 125.

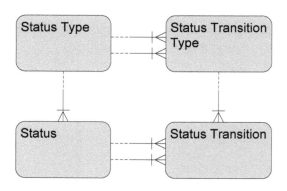

Figure 125 – Status Transition Rule Based model

Milestones

Milestones are very similar to Status Transitions.

However, there are subtle differences that mean Milestones are more applicable to certain types of activities in the Real World.

Status Transitions tend to be driven by (ad-hoc) individual events whereas Milestones are more to do with processes reaching a certain level of outcome or delivery.

To try to characterise them; Status Transitions are well suited to Workflows and Milestones are more relevant to Project style activities.

It is because Milestones allow us to record the attainment of a particular stage in progression that they are particularly useful to record progress for:

1.   Agreements between Parties

2.   Project and Programme progressions

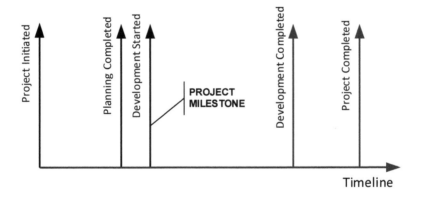

Figure 126 – Project Milestones

The model fragment in figure 127 will allow us to record the Milestones for a Project.

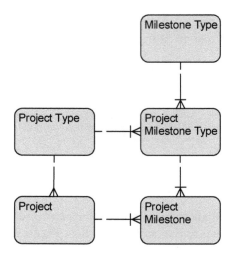

Figure 127 – Milestone pattern model[54]

Notice that there is no Milestone Transition defined using this model. However, by adding the multiple Relationships as per the Status Transition model in figure 125, we could prescribe Milestone Transitions.

Since Milestones are more relevant to planned types of activity executions, standard Attributes for the Milestone Entity often include the:

- Planned Attainment Date

- Actual Attainment Date

Phases

We have seen how Milestones allow us to record the attainment of various levels produced by a set of activities.

What they don't model is the duration of the processes that lead up to the Milestone attainment. Where the data model needs to represent the process activities starts and ends, we can build on the Effective Date Tool we acquired earlier. However, in this class of activities, their 'currency' represents a Phase.

This is illustrated in figure 128.

---

54 Hopefully you will be able to spot Rule Based Modelling in this fragment.

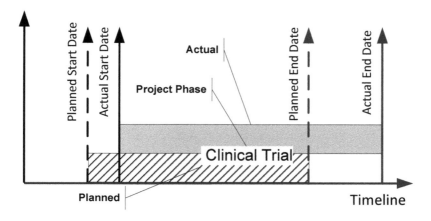

Figure 128 – Phases illustration

Similarly to the Milestone model, Phases tend to be associated with planned activities and so have the planned and actual Attributes. But also they have starts and ends. This gives rise to four standard Attributes for the Phase Entity being included:

- Planned Start Date

- Actual Start Date

- Planned End Date

- Actual End Date

The model fragment that is a standard pattern for this Tool is illustrated in figure 129.

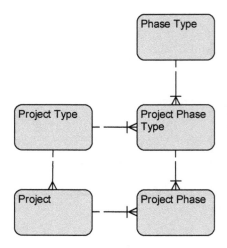

Figure 129 – Project Phase model

Of course, now we have the Milestone and Phase patterns, decisions will need to be made as to whether they are interrelated in your model. Are there key Milestones that are related to Phases and indicate their start or end? Are there Milestones that are related to, but are not Phase-changing Milestones?

These considerations will depend on the specific uses of the data for which your models are being constructed.

Effective Date Lifecycles

One of the simplest Lifecycle models that we can use is based upon the Effective Date pattern that we have seen in an earlier section in this chapter.

In this simple model, the elements related to a key headline Entity at any point in time are determined by their Effective Date Attributes. To illustrate this let's think about a multiple vehicle Insurance Policy.

Let's imagine the timeline for a specific for Car Insurance Policy as illustrated in figure 130.

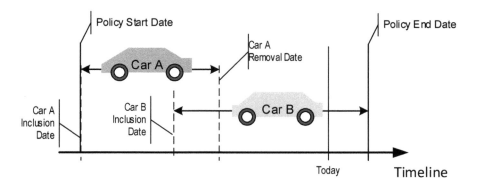

Figure 130 – Simple Effective Date Lifecycle

Car A was included for coverage at the Policy inception. Some while later Car B was added and a short while after this, Car A was removed from the Policy.

This Policy Lifecycle can be represented by simply using our Effective Date Tool and applying this Tool to all of the relevant components of the Policy that can vary over time.

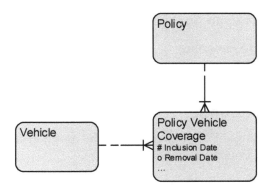

Figure 131 – Simple Effective Date Lifecycle model

Lifecycle Versioning

Many organisations use data that is governed by complex definitions of Products, Services or Terms and Conditions.

These headline level Entities can have Lifecycles that are typified by Versions of the same Entity instance. In this type of data scenario, an explicit Entity Version is typically the actual point of focus for the Relationships with other Entities. These other Entities are primarily the detailed Normalised structures that fully represent the entire high level Entity. For example, when we think of a Policy, it is the Policy Version that is typically of importance, rather than the Policy Entity itself. All the details about the Policy can be changed as it goes through a Version Lifecycle, and so most of the related detail Entities should relate explicitly to the *Version* of the Policy.

Figure 132 illustrates a simple model fragment to illustrate this concept.

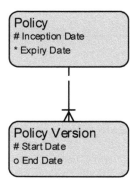

Figure 132 - Entity Lifecycle Versioning

There are several variations on this modelling approach which include:

- Relationship Versioning
- Full Entity Versioning

Relationship Versioning

Let's see how the simple Policy example as illustrated in figure 130 would be represented using a Policy Version approach.

In the Real World the Vehicles attached to a Policy would get included in a particular Version and if required removed from a subsequent Version.

For each Entity that is related to the Policy Version Entity, we will require two Relationships between it and the Policy Version; one that records the inclusion Version and the other to record the Version in which its definition was removed.

The pattern for this is illustrated in figure 133

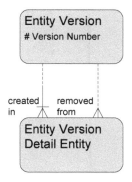

Figure 133 – Relationship Versioning Lifecycle model

This pattern works well where the majority of the Detail Entities' data does not change between subsequent versions.

Figure 134 illustrates the way that the Detail Entity data for our Car coverage will vary over the Policy Version Lifecycles.

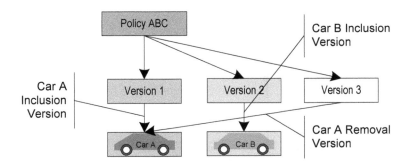

Figure 134 - Relationship Versioning Lifecycle illustration

The Car coverage data will be recorded once only and will have a 'created in' Version of 'Version 1' for Car A and 'Version 2' for Car B.

Car A will also be linked via its 'removed from' Relationship to Policy 'Version 3'.

Figure 135 illustrates the data model fragment to support this.

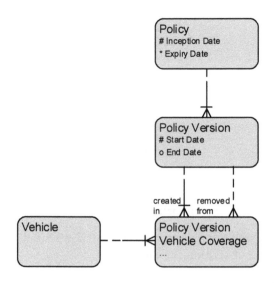

Figure 135 – Relationship Versioning Lifecycle model

Full Entity Versioning

This model is subtly different from the preceding one.

The Detail data instances that remain associated to the Entity (in this case the Policy) get repeated as illustrated in figure 136.

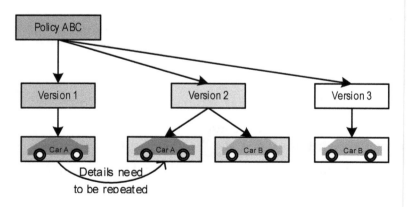

Figure 136 – Full Entity Versioning Lifecycle illustration

So even though Car A coverage details did not change when Car B got added to the Policy, these details would need to be repeated into the next Policy Version.

The data model fragment to support this is illustrated in figure 137.

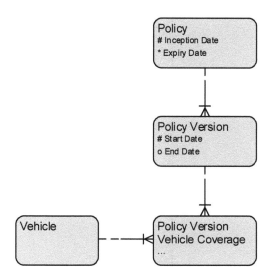

Figure 137 – Full Entity Versioning Lifecycle model

For most examples in the Real World this simple approach is highly effective. However, where only minor changes occur for each variation on the original instance and there are a lot of these, the downside is that the data is repeated over and over again, despite very little of it changing.

The Deliverables

15: Data Model Development Approach

Introduction

We have now filled up our Toolkit with Tools that we can use to create and maintain our data models.

This means that we are at the stage where we are ready to find out about the *process* of data modelling.

You may be working on existing models or be creating one or more data models from scratch, but the questions remain the same; where on earth do you start? And what exactly do you need to do?

This chapter is dedicated to answering these questions.

Depending on the reason for your data modelling, you may need to consider how its activities are co-ordinated with other concurrent activities. The meshing of these activities may be key to the success of both. This chapter also describes how the data modelling activities need to be integrated within a Project or Programme.

The Embryonic Data Model

The best place to start to create a data model, is at the beginning, if possible.

The beginning *should* be to create a high level scoping data model of what is required[55]. This will help by bounding the data landscape that your models need to define.

This can actually be done very rapidly.

It will have very few Entities, perhaps a dozen, and will consist of mainly the Entities that strike you in the very first few days of starting your modelling work.

---

55 This can be incorporated into, or referenced from within, the Data Modelling Approach document to help to define the data scope.

Obvious examples of high level Entities that are found in many models are:

- Person and Organisation

- Location

- Product

- Order

These initial, very high level scoping data models are commonly called Conceptual Data Models, although they can sometimes also be called:

- Business Data Models

- High Level Logical Models

- Level Zero Logical Models

These models are extremely important for all sorts of reasons, and in particular to:

- ensure the overall coherence of a family[56] of data models

- define the data scope

- assist with high level communication

When building this Conceptual Data Model, a lot of ground can be covered very quickly without getting caught up too much in the detail. However, the Relationships between the High Level Entities still need to stack up. This is because this model will form the basis of all the other models, and in particular will drive the definition of the Logical Data Models.

Therefore, you can't take short cuts and you must use the 3-D modelling techniques introduced earlier.

As an example of the Conceptual Data Model, figure 138 illustrates the Organisation and Person High Level Entities that might be found in one.

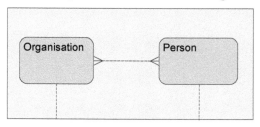

Figure 138 - Organisation and Person Conceptual Model

56   More detail is provided on this concept of a family of data models in chapter 20.

Notice that at this level it is quite legitimate for the Relationships between the Entities to be represented as M:M Relationships. This is because we have not yet started the detailed analysis and process of Normalisation that will allow us to resolve them.

With so few Entities and such a small amount of detail, we can complete the Conceptual Data Model very rapidly. But we are not going to ignore it upon completion, because it will be used as the basis for the Logical Data Model. This model will be started using the same high level Entities and Relationships but will start to resolve the Relationships and Normalise the Entities using the Tools we have already acquired.

This Normalisation process will produce a lot more Entities and for all of these we need to flesh out their detail as described in the next section.

Logical Data Models

Logical Data Models are the fully Normalised models derived from the Conceptual Data Model.

By evolving the Logical Data Models from the Conceptual Models, we will ensure that there is coherence across these two important levels.

> *Key Point 76*   *The Enterprise Conceptual Data Model __must__ form the basis from which the Enterprise Logical Data Models are developed.*

Figure 139 illustrates the progress from the Conceptual Data Model to the Logical Data Model.

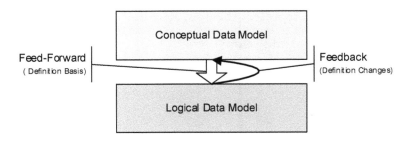

Figure 139 – Conceptual Data Model as the basis for Logical Data Models

The key feature of this schematic is the feed forward arrow. This indicates the transfer of the understanding and high level definition of Entities. This flow of definitions is required to ensure coherence between these two levels of data models.

Figure 139 also indicates that there are feedback loops from the transition and subsequent work on the Logical Data Model. This feedback can arise as new understanding is revealed by the more detailed discovery and decision making activities.

The Logical Data Model should also be seen as a foundational model upon which other Artifacts of the organisation's Enterprise Data Models[57] should be based, notably the:

1. Canonical Models

2. Normalised Physical Data Models

3. De-normalised or Dimensional Models

4. Data Dictionaries

The Data Modeller must resolve all Many to Many relationships in a Normalised Logical Data Model. This is because, if they remain unresolved, they can hide other Entities and structures that record data upon which the organisation is dependent.

To illustrate the preceding point, let's follow a simple example of the transition of a Conceptual Data Model into a Logical Data Model focussing on the way that the M:M Relationships are resolved.

Conceptual Data Models - unresolved Many to Many Relationships

In the fragment of a Conceptual Data Model illustrated in figure 140, it is perfectly acceptable to represent the M:M Relationships between:

* Research Study and Person

* Person and Interaction

---

57   See chapter 20 for more detail on what these are.

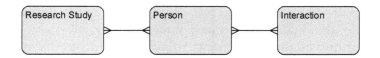

Figure 140 - M:M Relationships in a Conceptual Data Model[58]

But we have learned that the M:M Relationship Type is unacceptable in the Normalised Logical Data Models. We have also learned of a standard resolution for these. The next section describes the transition of this model fragment from the Conceptual Data Model to the Logical Data Model.

Logical Data Models - resolved Many to Many Relationships

Whilst we may have quite a few M:M Relationships in our first stages of creating a Logical Data Model, we know that these must ultimately be resolved.

We have defined a standard resolution Tool that will provide a first-cut resolution for M:M Relationships, so we can just use this and move on - right?

Often this is the extent of the analysis involved in the resolution process; a simple Intersection Entity is added to replace the M:M Relationships 'by default'. Once this has been created it is *assumed* to be correct and attention turned to other matters.

However, let's use the example in figure 141 and see what the outcome would be if we simply used this approach.

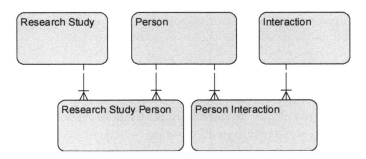

Figure 141 - Simple first-cut M:M Relationships resolution

Although our resolution Tool was used to provide a first-cut as illustrated in figure 141, further analysis should then be carried out.

58 Although you can't use the crow's feet as an indicator for the how you need to lay out the Conceptual Data Model, you can still use the Volumetrics to act as a guide. The low volume Entities should be placed top left and high volume Entities bottom right as much as possible. See figure 35 as a guide.

As a consequence of such analysis, the original M:M Relationships reveal a *data structure* that records the way that People are related to Research Studies. For example, this additional detailed understanding, allows us to link the Interaction Entity to the correct new Attendance Entity in the model.

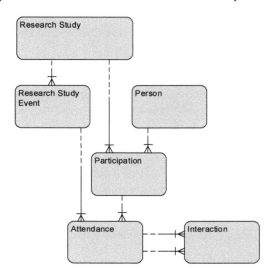

Figure 142 – Fully Resolved M:M Relationship[59]

What we have witnessed here is that although a useful Tool, our M:M Relationships Resolution Tool should not be assumed to provide the final structures by default. Whatever the outcomes are from using any of our Tools, they still require critical review.

In this example, several key Entities and their Relationships would not have been revealed without assessing the output from our Tools.

Logical Data Model Subject Areas

Because large, complex Logical Data Models may not be feasible to complete in a single concerted effort, we need to make them more achievable by carving up the effort into smaller bite sized chunks.

By starting with the Conceptual Data Model, it is possible to independently begin developing individual areas of the model in more detail. These make sense to develop as, Subject Area Logical Data Models.

But how do we decide what constitutes a Subject Area?

I would start with the High Level Entities in the Conceptual Data Model. A

---

59 Notice the inclusion of Rule Based Modelling structures here!

Subject Area would typically contain only a few of the High Level Entities contained in this.

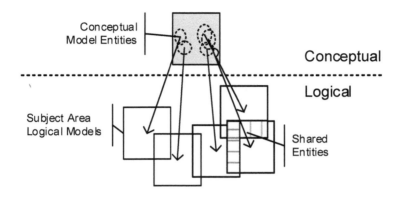

Figure 143 - Developing Subject Area Logical Data Models

Figure 143 illustrates how the high level or Conceptual Data Models can be used as the basis on which to derive the more complex lower level Subject Area Logical Data Models.

> *Key Point 77*   *Subject Areas in Logical Data Models can be based on a handful of the Entities from the Conceptual Data Model.*

Notice in figure 143 that there are shared Entities.

What we mean by shared, is that they occur in more than one Logical Data Model Subject Area. These shared Entities provide the linking structures *across* the individual Subject Areas.

For example, a Person Role may appear in many of the Subject Area models. The inclusion of these shared Entities ensures that the Subject Area models are linked and therefore guarantees coherence across the entire data model.

Let's look at an example of how this can work using part of a Conceptual data model as in figure 144.

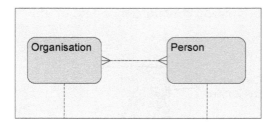

Figure 144 - Organisation and Person Conceptual Model

These two high level Entities can then be developed into a more detailed representation in a single Party Subject Area as shown in figure 145 below.

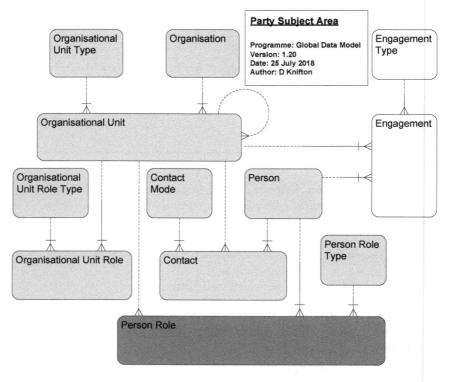

Figure 145 - Party Subject Area Model

Notice in figure 145 that the Person Role Entity is highlighted. This Entity is shared with another Subject Area as illustrated in figure 146.

This provides an example of how the Subject Areas need to link together in order to create the overall Logical Data Model – think of the way that individual jigsaw pieces interlock to provide the overall picture.

Key Point 78   *Entities that are shared across more than one Subject*
Area allow us to fit together the different parts of the
model and thus create a single coherent data model.

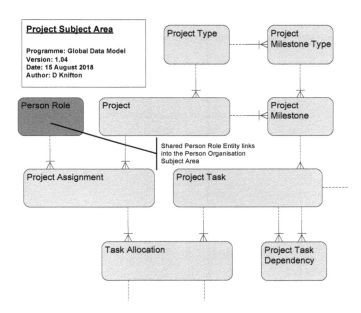

Figure 146 - Shared Entities between Subject Areas

If you have a Subject Area Data Model that does not incorporate at least one Entity that is shared with another Subject Area, then this suggests you need to question why this Subject Area is not linked to any of the other parts of the model.

Subject Area Conceptual Data Models

For some organisations that have a large number of High Level Entities, the Conceptual Data Models themselves may be created as separate High Level Subject Areas, for example, for Finance, or Order Fulfilment.

These present the overall landscape with a reduced number of Entities in each Conceptual Subject Area. As a result this makes the entire data landscape far easier to consume for stakeholders. These will still need shared Conceptual Entities such as Client, in order to make them coherent.

Stakeholders' Relationships With Data Models

What has been conspicuously absent from the discussion so far, is the way that the key stakeholders interact with the data models.

Earlier it was stated that the data models *must* represent the collective understanding and agreed *meaning* of the data by the stakeholders of an organisation.

To the extent that the key stakeholders and SMEs are able to convey an accurate understanding of this, they need to have detailed input and be part of any of the data models' review processes.

Key Point 79 *The effective involvement of key stakeholders and SMEs is absolutely critical in defining and maintaining the data models*

Key Point 79, is illustrated by figure 147.

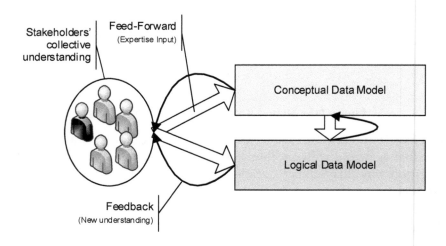

Figure 147 - Stakeholders relationships with data models

If data models are to be of maximum benefit for an organisation, processes that provide essential stakeholder input need to be created and *implemented*. This doesn't mean that we will see stakeholders poring over detailed data model micro-structures.

Nonetheless, their involvement must be effective if these data models are to be successful in transforming the data benefits for an organisation.

Notice also that in figure 147, feedback can take place from the models to the stakeholders. This can happen for many reasons, such as, when the modelling process has uncovered new patterns, domains or data structures, of which the stakeholders were previously unaware. Challenging assumptions and constraints articulated by stakeholders can also result in enhancing *their* understanding.

Data Models Development Profile

When data modelling, I have found that the technique generally follows the 80/20 rule, that is, 80% of the model can be defined with about 20% of the overall effort. This 80% proportion of the definition refers to; correctly modelling the majority of the Entities, their Relationships and their headline Attributes.

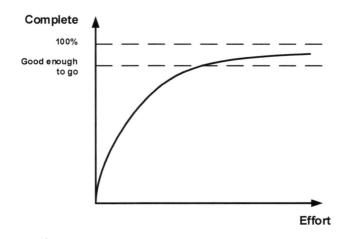

Figure 148 - Data modelling effort to completion profile

The chart in figure 148 illustrates a typical effort versus 'completeness'[60] profile of data modelling. What it shows is that the model progress can be rapid to begin with, as core Entities and their Relationships can be put together quickly[61]. What takes the majority of the time is; refining the understanding and resolving complex structures, providing comprehensive Attribution, and documenting the details.

---

60 What we mean by 'Complete' is interesting and is addressed in chapter 18.

61 I'm afraid that another point it illustrates, is that data models will *never* be a 100% perfect representation of the Real World.

The Data Modeller can develop the Enterprise Logical Data Model, by getting the structure correct with minimal effort and then complete the detail when there is an opportunity.
Such an opportunity may arise, for example, when a specific Project drives the need for a Subject Area of the data model to be fully defined, and can therefore provide the focus and funding for it.

What is also indicated in figure 148, is that from a construction timeline point of view, there is a decreasing return of benefit from additional effort being expended on the model. Once this plateau is reached, expending more effort may not yield sufficient benefit to the organisation to be worthwhile.

'Good Enough To Go'

When the plateau region of the data model effort in figure 148 is attained, it is at the point where the data model could be deemed to be *'Good enough to go'*.

This is an important point.

To be able to recognise when it has been reached requires careful judgement and a realistic appreciation that the data model will *never* be *perfect* or indeed finished.

Another way to decide whether this threshold has been reached is by detecting that although expending more effort is yielding *some* benefit, it is not adding *sufficient* benefit to justify any further delay of the model's consumption.

Do We Care?

Determining the point where we reach the 'Good enough to go' threshold of the data modelling process, provides a perfect example of when we should invoke the 'Do we care?' challenge. This challenge allows us to decide whether it is worth expending any more effort trying to unearth any further enhancements or deficiencies in the model.

In other words, will sufficient *benefit* be derived by any *extra effort* to justify it being expended?

However, be reassured that the 'Do we care?' principle is not about trying to avoid work, or an expression of indifference, or weariness, but rather about ensuring that the maximum benefit is delivered for a given amount of effort.

> **Key Point 80** *The 'Do we care?' challenge is extremely important in data modelling as it can be used to redirect effort that would deliver negligible benefit to activities that yield greater benefit, thus leading to better quality deliverables overall.*

Data Models And The Software Development Life-Cycle

Where data models are being developed in the context of a Project or Programme, the data modelling processes will need to be integrated with the overall effort. In this section we'll look at how to do this within the Software Development Life-Cycle (SDLC).

The SDLC approach is a standard way[62] of delivering Software deployments, often characterised as being a 'waterfall' approach.

The typical stages in this approach include:

1. Analysis – specifying Requirements

2. Design – defining the Solution

3. Development – creating Solution infrastructure

4. Testing – ensuring the developed Solution meets the Requirements

5. Deployment – implementing the Solution

Ideally, there should be an overlap of activities in the phases, so that for example, impediments to Development are fed back into the earlier stages.

Figure 149 illustrates that the Conceptual Data Models and the Normalised Logical Data Models need to have been started by early in the Analysis phase. Prior to the start of the Design phase, the Logical Data Models need to be at (or very close to) the 'Good enough to go' threshold of maturity. By the time any Physical Models are being developed, the Conceptual and Logical Data Models should be well past this stage and should be considered to have been 'completed'.

---

62 Although somewhat out of vogue at the moment.

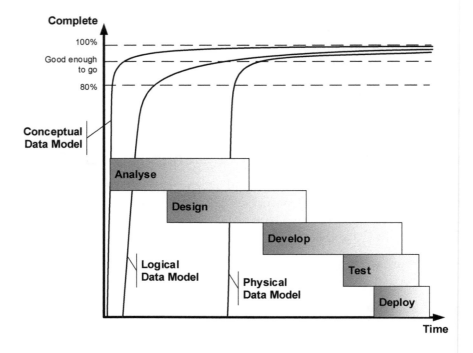

Figure 149 - Data modelling within SDLC

Notice that the trajectory at the start of each of the models is very steep.

For the Conceptual Data Models this is because they are relatively simple, so rapid progress can be made.

Because the Logical Data Model will be based upon the Conceptual Data Model, its initial Entities and structures are easily put together and, as a result, a rapid first-cut is possible.

Ideally a Normalised Physical Data Model should be largely based upon the Logical Data Model[63] and so can be constructed fairly much in an automated 'forward engineered' manner.

Notice though that if the subsequent models are started too early, then the whole effort can become mired in the process of constantly cross-referencing and re-factoring each of the model levels. These changes can arise, for example, due to new discoveries from the Design or Development.

---

63 For more detail on the transformation please refer to chapter 20.

Data Modelling Using An Agile Approach

The Agile Methodology is an alternative to the SDLC Waterfall approach described in the previous section. Instead of having sequential phases, it uses a series of iterative Sprints, the outcome of each of these feeding into the start of the next.

It promises a rapid delivery of first-cuts that can be very tempting for many organisations. This is especially true where the organisation has been badly burned by very large projects or programmes that adopted a waterfall approach but failed to deliver satisfactory developments - sometimes even after many years of work!

In my experience, the Agile approach can also work extremely well with large Data Migration projects. Even in these though, there may still be the need to create data models that act as a conformed organisation-centric definition of the data. These models can assist the transformation from the Source data to an idealised Target data specification.

Essentially, the Agile approach can be characterised as being a series of mini SDLC stages, each with processes that enforce feedback into earlier levels of specification. These can provide a successful way to deliver development projects, if the organisation has the appropriate culture and stakeholders have the correct expectations and experience.

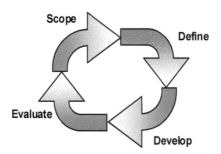

Figure 150 - The Agile Methodology Lifecycle

A simplified representation of the Agile development cycle is illustrated in figure 150.

In figure 151 the Agile cycle has been 'unfolded' to give a linear time line that the data modelling effort can be mapped to. What it shows is that we can actually view the modelling effort as simply a variation on the SDLC time line.

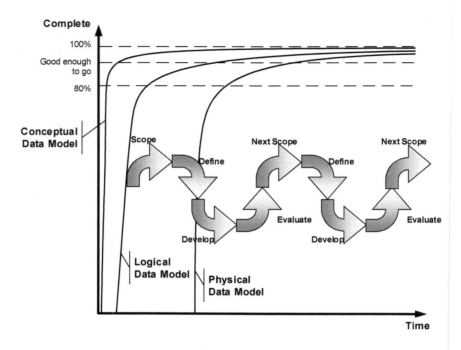

Figure 151 - Data Modelling within Agile Development

What it also makes clear is that the data models need to be developed to a significant level of maturity prior to Sprint 1.

In the same way as for the SDLC approach in the previous section, if the data models are not developed to a satisfactory degree of maturity, the whole Agile approach can flounder due to constant re-work of the data models in subsequent cycles.

There is also something else worth mentioning here and that is to do with the inherent conflict in developing the data models *within* the Agile cycles. Because of the nature of the Agile methodology, the underlying data models only need to support the immediate requirements to be deemed adequate.

What is missing from this approach to data model development is the big picture. As a result each iteration in the development of an Enterprise system may run into problems that are caused by Sprints only satisfying their sub-set of requirements.

Only recently I worked with a client on an Enterprise system development programme that attempted to develop the underlying data model using an Agile approach.

The resulting data model path is depicted on figure 152.

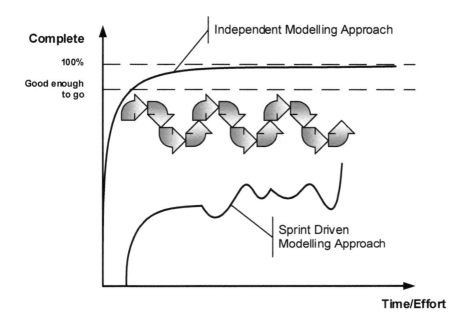

Figure 152 - Data Modelling in Agile Development

Initially there seemed to be rapid progress, but as each Sprint unfolded the amount of rework that was required meant that the model was nowhere near an Enterprise level of maturity overall.

There were a lot of data model structural problems and the data required a lot of 'fixing' before it could be extracted and used within other Enterprise systems. In addition, as each Sprint's re-factoring piled on the previous and the workarounds for the immature structures became more and more complex and were 'baked into the system'. As a result, the expense required made the chance of reworking the data model, and hence make the system truly an Enterprise system, ever more remote.

To avoid this outcome, it makes sense to develop the models independently and make them available at day 1. If this is possible, then the Sprint development work can proceed with a sound basis and the improvement in the deliverables can be dramatic.

Some organisations adopt a Sprint 0 to set up the infrastructure and create other pre-requisites for the subsequent Sprints. Therefore a possibility, is to start the data modelling effort during or, if possible, before this initiation Sprint. This should allow it to get to the point of 'Good enough to go' early enough in the Sprint cycles, to be stable and remove the need for substantial rework.

Rapid Active Data Modelling (RADM)

The earlier brief description of the 3-D data model development process seems a bit like a mixture of SDLC and Agile methodologies overall.

However, where mention of workshops or other sessions is made, it could be an option to use techniques that I call Rapid Active Data Modelling (RADM). If you are blessed with the right groups of stakeholders, then this style of modelling can be highly effective to develop data models from scratch *very* quickly *and* with a high degree of accuracy.

The tools for this activity are very basic. All you need are; yellow stickies, a whiteboard (or a glass partition), a sprinkling of enthusiasm and about half a dozen key stakeholders with *open minds*.

Step 1 – capturing the Entities

Make sure that your stakeholders each have a marker pen and a pad of yellow stickies. Typically pick a single Subject Area to work on and time box the effort to say an hour. Set the scene by describing the scope of the Subject Area to provide context for the activity and explain what you wish the stakeholders to do.

The simple instructions for the stakeholders should include:

1. Write down as many 'things' of significance within the Subject Area as they can think of

2. Make it clear that you are expecting one 'thing' per sticky

3. As they record each 'thing', they need to stick it up on the surface

Then ask all of the stakeholders to stand up and start recording the Entities!

If you have the right collection of stakeholders, what typically happens during this initial phase is a frenzy of interactions between them. For example, stakeholders want to see if someone else has already thought of the thing that they are thinking of, or is using a different name for the same thing and so on.

What can also happen is that participants from different areas of the organisation start to realise that the way they think about certain data elements is different, but through the RADM Sessions, they actually start to align their understandings of these!

At this initial stage, try not to judge the contributions too much, as this can create more hesitancy and introspection, leading to fewer contributions. However, as the facilitator, you might need to cajole participants from time to time, and also keep the group on track.

After a while there should be a lot of stickies!

Step 2 – reviewing the Entities

When the rate of contributions starts to subside and participants start to 'um…' and 'er…', it is time to review what people have contributed.

A part of this review will be to weed out any non-Entities e.g. Quarterly Sales Report. Also try to group things together that are the same, but have been named differently. These may well be valid Synonyms referring to the same Entity.

Get some sheets of paper and peel the stickies off the surface and stick them next to each other onto the paper.

Figure 153 – A yellow sticky stack of Entities

Where the same Entity is repeated using Synonyms, stick these together on top of each other.

Step 3 – Creating Relationships

Now using your own modelling skills and the methodical layout suggested earlier, start to return the stickies to the surface. But this time try to place Reference Entities at the top left and the Transactional Entities at the bottom right.

As you return the stickies, explore the Relationships of each Entity to the other Entities with the stakeholders in the group. This can be difficult to manage but will definitely flush out differing opinions very quickly.

If using a whiteboard or glass partition, you can draw up the Relationships using a whiteboard marker (making doubly sure it is not a permanent marker!).

It might not be possible to get the whole Subject Area finalised in a single session using this technique, but the ground covered can be amazing.

RADM advantages

Because RADM compresses all of the 3-D activities into one session, the advantages from using it can be phenomenal.

However, you really do need to have the correct culture and individuals to make this work.

The following advantages can accrue from using it:

1. Shortened data modelling time

2. Better quality data models

3. Consensus baked into the data models

4. Shared ownership and increased commitment from stakeholders

5. Skills transfer to stakeholders

6. Feedback of new understanding to stakeholders

7. Higher regard for the resultant data models and data modelling as a worthwhile endeavour for your organisation

Big Data and the Enterprise Data Models

This chapter is devoted to data model development and just before we leave it, we need to tackle the conundrum raised by Big Data adoption that was described in the Introduction. There, it was stated that accurate data models within an organisation's data scope, will remain true representations over extended periods of time. But, it was also noted that many people believe that with the advent of Big Data, data models are no longer useful, or even relevant and we should discard them.

Whilst I strongly contest this view, what is almost certain is that adopting Big Data will cause the Logical Data Models to be extended to support its new data realms.

A primary driver for organisations wanting to adopt Big Data, is the need to focus on external events and their consequent 'data vapour trails'. This is so that organisations can understand what is happening in their external operational environment. The typical example given, is that the organisation will be able to 'understand its customers more fully'. This example is supported by the evidence of organisations increasingly communicating messages and offerings to their customers that are highly attuned to the customer's specific profile.

Organisations that have started to embrace this external environmental data, must revisit any Enterprise Data Models that were built prior to this era. The earlier data models are characterised as being organisation-centric and introspective in their scope.

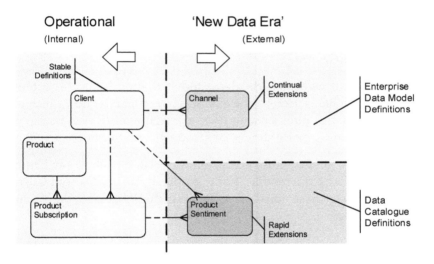

Figure 154 - Extended data model scope

Figure 154 is a simplified data model fragment that illustrates the three areas for the Enterprise Data Models to consider:

1. Operational Domains – existing

2. External Domains – extensions

3. Analysis Domains – highly volatile

Let's examine these in a little more detail in the following sections.

Operational Domains

The operational areas of the data models will remain largely unchanged (hopefully) - even in this new data era. This is because they reflect the internal operations of the organisation and, as we saw earlier, they should be mechanism-agnostic. In other words, even if the way we carry out activities becomes re-engineered, the data models should not require corresponding revisions.

Note that they may need to incorporate generic structures to support Localised or Extensible Attribution as described earlier on page 185. However, these concrete structures can provide extensibility without the need for us to constantly revamp the data model definitions.

External Domains

As we are aware, in the last few years many organisations have undergone a revolution to Digital Marketing. This is a good example in this new data-rich era, of the need for organisations to rethink the way that they interact with their operational environment.

The resulting refocus will cause the data models that underpin the interactive operations of our organisations to be extended to reflect the new mechanisms through which they can interact with their external worlds. For example new channels for Marketing, or fulfilment of Products and Services.

But notice that these new realms still need to be related back to key Entities in the Operational area of the models. For example, if we think about Customer Product Preferences, these must have Relationships back to the Customer and Product Entities.

Although the data world is changing rapidly, the volatility of these new data domains still takes place sufficiently slowly to justify the effort to define them in the Enterprise Data Models. Typically also, because they are of operational significance, they will have complex Relationships back into the Operational Domain's scope.

Analytical Domains

The third area of the data models is where the white heat of change prevails and the definitions within this scope will be highly volatile. As a result, they will almost certainly never be part of the Enterprise Data Models. Or, if they are, they are likely to be represented in generic, highly meta-data driven data structures that may result in their meaning being obscured.

And yet, we must catalogue them. This is so that their meaning can be shared by the consumers of the data analysis.

This raises the thorny question of where they will be catalogued.

This is definitely not an easy question to answer. You will have to find a way to disseminate the definitions of the data to the consumers, or prospective consumers. Possibly, for example, this could take the form of a dynamic catalogue within the reporting capability itself. But of course, this would limit the sharing of these meanings to a very small set of stakeholders. However, this may be a perfectly acceptable constraint. This is because, the people who will be interested in the analysis will be focussing purely from a strategic and operational improvement perspective. As a result, they will naturally only form a small part of the organisation's functions.

Again though, notice that for the vast majority of our organisations, these new insights are only relevant in the context of the data models' areas that we have already described in the preceding sections. This means that, at some level, they must still integrate with the preceding areas of the data models. Typically this determines that as a minimum, for example, they must have Relationships back into our Master Data domains.

16: Where to Start?
– The Engagement Process

Introduction

So far we have; developed a number of Tools, gained an understanding of the Processes and looked at the approaches allowing you to develop your data models.

But imagine now that you find yourself sitting at your desk pondering exactly what you are going to do to start these activities.

This chapter describes the Engagement Process which is the first phase of activities required for the development of your data models. Its purpose is to ensure that all of the necessary infrastructure and communication channels are set up. Establishing these will maximise the outcomes from the overall process, and minimise the effort expended on it.

The key outcomes from this process are to agree the timeframes and deliverables with all stakeholders.

There are four themes in this initial phase and these are to focus on:

1. Communication

2. Commitment

3. Agreement and Consensus

4. Scope

This chapter describes how these themes form the basis of the Engagement Process and therefore maximise benefit from the subsequent data modelling effort.

Creating The Engagement Process

The Engagement Process is the entry gatekeeper for the overall data modelling activities.

As soon as you embark upon a data modelling assignment, you will need to define your engagement approach. The first thing to do is to consider how formal this definition will need to be and thus how much effort to devote to the creation of it.

For example, is it appropriate to create shared formal documentation, or do you only need to document this process to the level that will help *you* think through the impending activities?

There is no prescriptive list of things that you *must* do to create this definition. You will need to think carefully about the culture of your organisation, as much as anything else, and tailor what you do to mesh with this. If you don't do this, you will definitely run the risk of the fruits of your labour becoming forgotten in a data model repository, instead of having a transformational impact on your organisation.

Data Modelling Approach document

I often use a technique of creating a Data Modelling Approach definition, even though sometimes I am the only consumer of it.

I find that documenting this helps me to frame my effort and clarifies the way forward in my mind. A template that can help you to put your own together forms appendix A.

Sometimes I have found that this definition can be completed in several hours, or, on occasion, has required several days of research and detailed specification.

You can start to create this document at the beginning of the Engagement Process by writing about half a page on the **Background**[64] to the data modelling effort. As we go through the following sections, there will be pointers to other sections that can be added to your document.

Standard Engagement Questions

For any specific data modelling effort it is worth using the following Standard Engagement Process questions to assist with the design of the Engagement Process:

1. Why?

2. Who?

3. What?

4. Where?

5. When?

6. How?

---

64   Refer to the Background section of the Data Modelling Approach template in appendix A.

The resolution of these questions should feed into a successful Engagement Process definition. What to consider when answering these questions is described in the following sections.

Why?

This question refers to 'Why are you engaged to carry out this data modelling effort in the first place?'

The answers to the 'Why?' question will help to determine the answers to many of the other questions in the list. For example, it should help to place the consumers, deliverables and the dissemination mechanisms into context within your organisation.

If you are creating a Data Modelling Approach document, once you are clear what the **Data Modelling Purpose** is, then record this within the Data Modelling Approach definition.

To help you to define the purpose, assess the drivers for your assignment. For example, a possibility is that the Logical Data Model will be used as the basis for defining a Physical Data Model for an Operational Data Store or a Data Warehouse.

It could be required to form the basis for agreeing the Domains across your organisation's data landscape, and be used within Domain Ratification processes defined in your MDM framework.

Or another possibility is that the Logical Data Model will lead to the definition of a Canonical Data Model that will ultimately form the basis of data exchange across the organisation's data landscape.

Who?

We have already established that data modelling cannot be carried out without the involvement of stakeholders. The input and commitment from the correct individuals can make the difference between success and failure. Engaging with the appropriate 'Who?' is therefore absolutely key to the success of your efforts.

If you have Data Governance and/or Master Data Management framework definitions in place, then you should think about including the key stakeholders within these areas.

In addition to these though, think about those who need to be involved who can carry out one of the following roles:

- Team Member
- Input SME
- Consumer
- Key influencer

The importance of these roles is described in the following sections.

Team Member

Discover the members of the Team/s you will be working with and find out how they may be able to support your data modelling effort.

Of special note are the information flows that may be facilitated by them. For example, can they:

- put you in touch with other key stakeholders?
- invite you to meetings to cover particular areas you need to research?

Input SME

The Input SMEs are those individuals whose knowledge and experience you will need in order to provide the essential information to successfully define your model.

Often those with the best grasp of what *really* happens, are close to the action and not necessarily those with senior managerial titles.

> **Key Point 81** *When trying to identify SMEs in an unfamiliar area of an organisation, the Data Modeller should never rely on titles to indicate an individual's level of expertise.*

Also don't forget that Input SMEs typically bring with them a sense of importance to the whole process that can help win the hearts and minds of other stakeholders.

Consumer

To ensure that your efforts produce deliverables that are appropriate to their consumers, you will need to find out who these are likely to be. This may be simple if the models are being developed for a specific Project or Programme, but not so simple if they are destined to become Enterprise Data Models.

If your models *are* destined for the Enterprise Architecture function, then you will need to consider the consumers as roles rather than individuals. For example, are the consumers likely to include; Data Architects, Development Teams, Solution Architects, Technical Architects?

Also consider that these stakeholders will need almost certainly require a different style of communication compared with operational stakeholders.

The Key Influencers

Key Influencers are the individuals who will help to ensure that your data models deliver a transformational impact on your organisation. These stakeholders may or may not already be in your list because they are in the preceding categories. However, including stakeholders who can carry out this role is absolutely critical to ensure your success.

The 'Who?' question regarding the Key Influencers may be a very simple question to answer if the models are purely Project based for example, as it is likely to be the Project Manager and/or the Development Manager. If however your models are destined for the Enterprise Architecture space, then you will need to consider who will champion their use.

If none of your existing list are able to carry out this role, then think who would be appropriate *evangelists* for the use of your data models. You will need to contact these individuals and try to gain their commitment to your cause.

If no-one is available for this role, you may need to promote the consumption of the data models yourself. I have found that in the absence of a better alternative, it is possible to make this approach successful. But its chances of success can be markedly improved by:

1. creating appropriate promotional material emphasising the benefits of the model adoption

2. contacting people in whose interest it is to improve delivery and minimise costs[65]

I have also created Engagement process definitions for the adoption of the

---

65   Often I have found that these people are very open to the suggestion that you may save them considerable effort and risk by having a lot of 'answers' already contained in your data models.

data models that can ease their use for implementations such as Development or Migration Projects.

The Who Template

I suggest that you use the following table[66] as a basis to help construct your stakeholder list.

Name	Title/ Role	Functional Area	Input SME	Team Member	Consumers	Key Influencer
Teresa Green	Head of Enterprise Architecture	EA	Y	N	Y	Y
Hans Offitzmien	Head of Finance UK/Eire	Finance	Y	Y	Y	Y

Once this table is completed, you can use it to see if you have adequate representation for all of your stakeholder areas. Refer back to it from time to time to ensure that all your communications are on track.

Where?

As a part of the Engagement Process you will need to identify where your sessions will be held. Importantly, can all, or indeed *any* of the sessions be face to face, or must at least some of them be virtual?

Although a lot *can* be achieved these days with a plethora of virtual communication tools, very few of these work seamlessly and none are the equivalent of being face to face in my experience.

For example, work out whether you will be using:

- Meeting rooms
- Conference calls

---

66 As per the Approach Template documentation.

- Video Conferencing
- Messaging groups

If at least some of these sessions are held face to face, then you will need to discover the physical location of your stakeholders to check whether there is any travel impact for them.

You may be working within a Global organisation and your stakeholders are spread across multiple geographical areas and you will need to figure out how to mitigate this.

Research the Venues

If you are new to the organisation, or to the locations, start to find out the characteristics of the venues. Of primary importance amongst these is their availability. Of course it is also important to be able to book these venues, and you may have to research the booking procedures if they are unfamiliar.

If you have no knowledge of the places where you plan to hold your sessions, then carry out as much research into these as possible. If the sessions are to be held in physical rooms, then try to go into them and check the; layout, realistic maximum number of people they'll hold and any broadcast capability.

If the locations are virtual, then trial the technology to become competent with at least its basic functionality beforehand. How many times have we been on calls where the first twenty minutes has been wasted because someone was trying to share their desktop? This waste of people's time can have quite a corrosive effect on stakeholder commitment and enthusiasm.

If there are projection facilities or screens in the rooms, then it is wise to check whether these work *before* the session starts. If using material through your own laptop for example, ensure that this can actually connect to the broadcast system. It can spell disaster for a session if you find you cannot hook up to the broadcast capability!

Tyranny of distance

Also think through the impact of stakeholders being located in different geographic areas. If travel is required, then consider timings for yourself, but also for other team members. So don't arrange a session to start at 8.30 a.m. if this means someone has to leave home at 4.30 a.m.!

In addition to different locations, you may also need to consider the time zone separation of stakeholders. Recently I was engaged to assist a Client with the definition of their Global data model which entailed working with two other Data Modellers. One of these was based in India, the other on the US East Coast. This led to us having very limited time when the three of us could meet together. To mitigate this required a lot of forward planning and flexibility of the individuals to work at non-standard hours!

What?

Referring to the Purpose paragraph you created for the 'Why?' section of your Data Modelling Approach definition and start to evaluate the 'What?' of the scope that the data models will cover.

Even if the data models are destined to become Enterprise Data Models, they may not have the entire Enterprise scope. They may be limited to specific High Level Subject Areas such as; Financial, Operations or Product Definition areas, for example.

The 'What?' is one of the most difficult questions to answer with any degree of certainty.

Reviewing the immediate requirements may help bound the scope, but Data Modellers always need to consider just beyond this. It is important to do this to verify that what lies beyond the boundary is definitely out of scope.

This bounding of the scope is illustrated by figure 155.

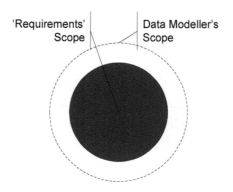

Figure 155 - Data Modellers scope boundary

At the same time, though, obviously you can't model the world!

So where do you stop?

This question is really the application of the 'Do we care?' challenge. This challenge needs to be raised at the boundary of the scope. Use the Data

Modelling Approach definition to record the **In Scope** and **Out of Scope** areas for your data modelling process.

Use the input from the other stakeholders to confirm these high level In Scope and Out of Scope definitions *at the start* of the process!

Key Point 82 *Data Modellers always need to bound the scope and need to consider what lies just beyond it to verify that it is out of scope.*

When?

The 'When?' question needs to be evaluated to ensure success but can also be very tricky to answer.

Create some rough timelines with significant milestones marked on it to help to form the overall shape of the Process. You don't want to run out of time for critical review sessions!

There are two major aspects that may constrain the timing of what the Data Modeller needs to organise:

1. External Processes
2. SME/Venue availability

These are described in more detail in the following sections.

External processes

Referring to the figures 149 and 151 in chapter 15, we saw that the Logical Data Models need to reach a threshold of maturity before any dependent project processes are started. This means that the data modelling processes would need to mesh with the overall Project Plan.

Therefore see when these are required to be at the 'Good enough to go' stage of maturity and work backwards from these to create your own delivery milestones.

SME/venue availability

Find out holiday schedules and other availability factors for your key stakeholders and especially SMEs. To find that one is going on sabbatical for six months right at the start of your schedule can severely compromise your ability to deliver your data model successfully.

Also make sure that if you are using physical venues for your meetings that these are going to be available throughout your modelling effort.

How?

At some point the mechanics of recording the outputs from the data modelling effort will need to be considered. At the beginning of the Engagement Process it is a good idea to think through the 'How?' of this.

To an extent, whether you like it or not, this will shape what you deliver. For example, what are the mechanisms involved in recording and disseminating your data models? Are there specific modelling tools and repositories that you need to gain access to, and familiarity with?

Communication Culture

Discover the way that the culture within your organisation affects communication. In chapter 3, we learned that the data models need to be integrated with the culture of the organisation. In the same way, the data modelling *processes* need to be aligned with its culture too.

In other words, does everything have to be documented carefully *prior* to any interaction, using documents that are version controlled and stored in a document repository? Or, is most of what needs to be achieved presentable through slides and recorded through informal meeting notes.

Are quick follow-up phone calls with key stakeholders permissible, or does everything have to be channelled through formal sessions where *every* stakeholder needs to be present whether or not its subject is of *any* interest to them.

Modelling and Enterprise Tools

Think through how you will disseminate your data models within the organisation. Is there an Enterprise tool in which you will need to create and maintain your data models?[67]

If the tools that will be used are unfamiliar to you, then set aside some time to get up to speed with them.

---

67   See Model Dissemination in chapter 19

For first-cuts, I would strongly suggest that you don't use software tools at all; instead use whiteboards. Whiteboards enable the creation and rapid restructuring of the data model and, as a result, structures can be created and refined in minutes that would otherwise take hours using a modelling tool.

In addition to the rapid prototyping of model structures, I am a strong believer in the power of whiteboards for guiding and aligning stakeholders during all sessions. Therefore, make sure that there are whiteboards *and pens* available in your venues.

Of course don't forget that there are virtual whiteboards available for virtual sessions.

Access permissions

Make sure that you and any other relevant stakeholders, have appropriate access privileges to any reference locations such as modelling tools or document management repositories. The allocation of these privileges may require a long lead time, so often you need to refer to your stakeholder list and start the process of gaining appropriate privileges for them as soon as you can.

Data Governance and Master Data Management Frameworks

The elephant in the room here is the distinct likelihood that you will have to mesh your modelling effort with an existing Data Framework. Whether this is a Data Governance Framework or Master Data Management Framework makes little difference in reality. Either way there will still be defined processes that your data modelling activities will need to follow.

So at what level of maturity are the framework definitions within which you will need to work?

If there is no formal Data Governance Maturity Model in place, then you may have to carry out a very rough assessment yourself.

If the Data Governance Framework is not mature, then consider that *you* might need to create or augment processes to make your data model better assimilated by the organisation.

Planning Your Data Modelling

Okay, so now we have established the Engagement Processes, we are ready to move on to the next stage which is to plan our data modelling processes.

We have already established that the involvement of stakeholders is crucial to create a successful data model and this, if nothing else, should mean that there needs to be some degree of planning of the overall process.

Planning activities

Once you have a reasonable idea of the overall landscape and the constraints that you face, it is time to start planning the activities. To construct a timeline and set of milestones to guide you through the overall process, you can use the information that you have to hand as a result of answering the Standard Engagement Questions listed in the previous section.

The rough timeline should be defined as it will be extremely beneficial. It should consider the following:

1. Deliverables

2. Milestone dates

3. Effort available

4. Resource/Venue availability

Unfortunately, because of the very nature of stepping into the 'unknown', the initial timeline definition cannot be too rigid. Sometimes organisations apply pressure to book a schedule of stakeholder workshops months in advance. This *can* be done but is unlikely to be fruitful.

To maximise their benefit, the sessions need to be timed to occur at appropriate points in the 3-D data modelling process. I also suggest that a 'little and often' approach is most effective for scheduling meetings.

Create a **Timeline** section in the Data Modelling Approach document to record the timeline that you define and use this to assess your dependencies on stakeholders and venues.

You may wish to have a separate section in your plan for each major Subject Area. For each of these you can start to plan the:

- Initial Engagement session

- Discovery sessions

- Consolidation feedback sessions

- Closure sessions

17: Data Modelling In 3-D
– Discover, Decide And Define

Introduction

By now you will have already have got your understanding of the overall data modelling process to the point where it is worthwhile holding the initial Discovery Sessions!

You will have executed the Engagement Process which will have produced the following deliverables:

- Engagement with relevant stakeholders

- Agreement on the scope and deliverables

- A Plan of the activities

- Creation of any necessary infrastructure

This chapter describes the actual mechanics of the data modelling 3-D Processes that will allow you to achieve your objectives by carrying out the following activity types:

- Discover

- Decide

- Define

These activities are so intimately linked that they act together to form a single cohesive set of required activities to define your data models. However, each of them has its own distinctly different characteristics from the others. It is these characteristics that are described in the following sections.

Discover

The Discover set of activities comprise the questioning component of data modelling.

Their aim is to extract the raw information that you will mould into the definitions of your data models using the other two 3-D activities.

> **Key Point 83** *The Discover activities unearth the raw content that feeds into the Decide and Define activities of the overall 3-D data modelling process.*

To be successful the discover activities must be just that - *active*.

Exchanging emails and documents will never succeed in delivering the understanding, nor the commitment and goodwill that are key to the data modelling process.

At some point, you will need to meet the stakeholders even if this is only virtually.

Active collaboration by the Data Modeller is key, since passively reading requirement documents will never reveal any of the <u>absent constraints and assumptions</u>. Engagement with stakeholders through activities, often yields otherwise hidden nuggets of understanding through 'off the cuff' remarks and unstructured conversations and anecdotes.

Carry out preliminary research

Some of what the data model will comprise will already have been Discovered and Defined within the organisation. There will almost certainly be fragments of the information that you require already in existence.

These may be well organised in a documentation repository of some nature that you can access. However, it is more likely that they will be dispersed across the intranet and possibly even located on the internet. Make use of these, coupled with initial conversations and briefings, to start to sketch out the landscape in which the data models will be formed.

This research may be assisted by the creation of an informal Conceptual Data Model[68] in the very earliest stages of the 3-D Process.

Process rather than Artifacts

Artifacts are normally seen as the way to communicate understanding, but is this true?

Artifacts *do* provide a communication tool, but when we think about the way that they communicate ideas, we can see that they are far from perfect for

---

68   For more detail on this please see page 211.

this purpose. We wouldn't dream of holding modelling sessions where the stakeholders play 'Chinese Whispers'. That is, one stakeholder whispering their understanding of the topic to the next, who then whispers their take on what they just heard to the next stakeholder and so on.

Yet when it comes to many processes within organisations, this is exactly the equivalent approach that we use. The author of an Artifact produces it and then disseminates it to others who try to gain the original understanding that the author had. This is illustrated by figure 156.

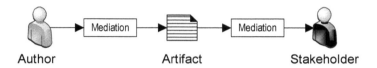

Author **Artifact** **Stakeholder**

Figure 156 – Communication by Chinese Whispers!

However, if you hold sessions to review Artifacts, then you are able to ensure that stakeholders gain the understanding that ideally the Artifacts *should* contain.

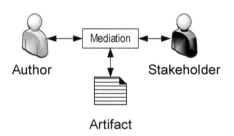

Author **Stakeholder**

Artifact

Figure 157 – "Ah! Now I get it."

The Data Modeller needs to use __processes__ rather than relying on __Artifacts__ to align stakeholders with the data modelling outcomes. This will bring them 'on the journey', and also results in collective ownership. These factors will ensure the easier assimilation of your data models.

Discovery Sessions style

To discover information you will need to engage with those who have best knowledge of it. Some of this discovery is possible to achieve through conversations, either in person or by phone. But at some stage early on, it is a good idea to hold formal sessions.

These can also help to set the tone and convey the importance of the work.

For the initial formal sessions, I would suggest having only a small number of stakeholders at each. Apart from the obvious discovery outcomes, use these sessions to assess your stakeholders. Try to gauge their attitudes, experience and possibly their own agendas. This will pay big dividends in any subsequent (larger) sessions, as you will be better placed to facilitate these more successfully.

Another advantage offered by holding these smaller initial sessions is that it may well be a lot easier for you to make rapid progress without it being hindered by group dynamics.

Discovery is just that, so in these initial sessions always ask 'Open' questions, for example, 'What is …?', or 'Could you provide examples of ..?'

Key Point 84   *Always use an 'Open' questioning style in the initial Discovery Sessions.*

There is another element to the open questioning style to consider. It will signal that you respect the opinions of the stakeholders, which will encourage them to have an honest and open style of responses. This will pay big dividends by facilitating better stakeholder communication in the longer term.

Try to also avoid 'Closed' questions such as 'I have a list of the Types here. Can you confirm ….?'

Closed questioning by contrast tends to imply that you already know the answers. This can trigger defensive responses and even lack of commitment to the Discovery processes.

You will need to prepare a number of questions prior to these first sessions. These will ensure that the sessions remain focussed and do not run out of steam and therefore lose momentum.

On the other hand, try to avoid being overly prescriptive in your questioning and *never* lead the witness in the initial sessions, as you don't yet know what you don't know! This means that you mustn't inadvertently bound the scope of the discussions too tightly.

> **Key Point 85** *Avoid being too prescriptive in questioning in the early stages as you don't yet know what you don't know!*

By-products from holding these sessions will be to build:

- the stakeholders' understanding of the objectives of the data modelling sessions

- rapport with the stakeholders

Create a relaxed and open atmosphere in the sessions and encourage a positive, non-judgmental approach from everyone.

Often stakeholders can feel that the sessions are an opportunity to let off steam about the problems that they face in their daily work. If you encounter this, try to be supportive but redirect such interactions to become a positive focus for the sessions. To do this, use phrases such as 'Hmm that doesn't sound good. But hopefully by getting useful outcomes from these sessions we can start to ...'

Always provide positive feedback for contributions and provide support for those who are not confident in group situations; those who are the most vocal are not always those with the best contributions!

Echo and Replay

Even in the first Discovery sessions, always check what you think is being communicated using the Echo and Replay technique.

This relies on echoing back what you think was just conveyed by other stakeholders, or getting others to replay what they think you have just communicated to them.

> **Key Point 86** *Echo and Replay can be used to establish that effective communication has taken place with common understanding and agreement.*

Also use this technique in emails or other similar communications, always summarise the significant outcomes from sessions and *always* invite correction in these.

Discovery Session profile

You should consider defining the following elements for each session:

- Session purpose
- Participant list
- Introductions

Set the Purpose of the Session

Try to ensure that the sessions have tightly defined purposes.

So, for example the purpose might be to:

- 'Define the data requirements for setting up a new Client'
- 'Review the high level Product definitions in the Enterprise Conceptual Data Model'

Always think through the agenda for the meeting and ensure that this is purely focussed on the purpose, and include it in the meeting invitation itself.

At the start of the meeting; state the objectives, set any context and for the first sessions, explain the overall purpose of the data modelling effort. Always make sure that the stakeholders are comfortable with the purpose before getting into the detail of the session.

Participant list

Try to ensure that the participants have a homogeneous profile.

For example, don't mix highly technical stakeholders in meetings with senior managerial people from the organisation's Operational side, without thinking carefully exactly what the session objectives are.

Obviously the stakeholders need to be well aligned with the purpose and so making sure that this is tightly focussed, will also help make it easier to closely align the participants.

If you are not familiar with any stakeholders prior to the session, try to find out some basic information about them. A quick phone call to invite them personally can pay big dividends in this regard.

Introductions

Make sure that the participants know one another and, if not, are introduced at the start of the session. If few of the stakeholders know each other in any of the sessions, use the standard technique of getting everyone to introduce themselves to the group.

Conflict Resolution

Often for the attendees for the sessions you will need to invite people who have strong opinions and opinions that may diverge from other outspoken participants.

These fault lines can be exposed during your discovery sessions. As the facilitator it is important not to lose control of the session!

But how do you stop these interpersonal disputes de-railing your efforts?

You may need to calm the situation down[69] and realign everyone with the purpose of the session. Always acknowledge that there *are* differences of opinion, but emphasise that this is not the time or place to resolve these.

Stay neutral and never get dragged into these disputes yourself.

Stakeholder commitment

An aspect to consider in your Engagement Process is that, although *we* believe in the pre-eminence of the data model, not everyone will share our belief, or indeed our enthusiasm.

For some stakeholders, it may not be seen as worthwhile use of their valuable time to define an understanding that they believe they already have, simply for you to create data models from which they can see no possible benefit!

You need to consider what benefits could accrue from such stakeholders' involvement and communicate these to them. Often an appeal to their sense of 'good citizenry' by helping you to get a clear and accurate picture of the organisation's data can work. But you will also need to communicate a wider organisational benefit that will improve their own work-related experience.

Part of the challenge here may be that the culture in your organisation has a classic Business/IT divide.

69   Hopefully not! But these situations do occur.

Due to its historic IT Development focus, data modelling can be considered by many to sit on the IT side. And yet its inputs *must* come from the operational side.

If this is the case, you need to consider how to build bridges that will overcome this division. In my experience a lot can be achieved by firstly candidly acknowledging the existence of such a division and then assure the operational stakeholders that it is *their* input that will form the basis of the data models. Make it clear that the deliverables will be used to improve the operational side of the organisation and this can be an effective bridge building technique.

Example dialogue

Here is a brief snippet that could have occurred in one of the many sessions that I have held over the years.

"OK, so can you tell me a little more about the Marketing Campaign term I hear everyone talk about?"

"Well yes. Um, when we get to hear about a new opportunity then we need to meet to discuss how we will mount a campaign to stimulate interest in the market for it. A group of us will typically meet and decide what channels and rough timelines will be needed.

If the opportunity is small, then the next stage will be to get a Digital Marketing team up to speed with the details and they will start to put together material and Marketing collateral straight away...."

Even in this very brief snippet, we have enough information to make a quick sketch of part of the data model for this Marketing area.

Create first-cuts

You may want to sketch out first-cuts in the sessions themselves. This has a key advantage of gaining immediate feedback whilst you have the benefit of the stakeholders' present and focussed.

Equally, you may not wish to, because you feel that this will distract stakeholders and de-rail the open responses that you are getting.

Whatever you do, do not use a modelling tool for these first-cuts! It will be far too slow.

Instead think about using whiteboards, virtual whiteboards or even a sheet of paper to quickly sketch out ideas[70].

Using the outcomes from the preceding example transcript fragment above, we already have enough information to start to list out some key Entities and their first-cut Relationships.

Figure 158 could have been the rough data model sketch made immediately after this session.

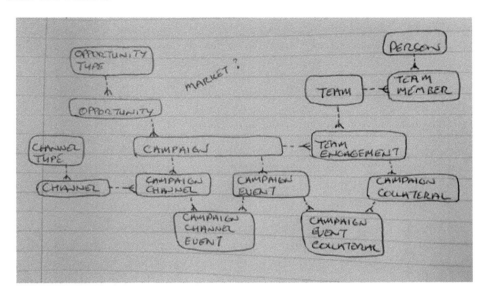

Figure 158 – First-cut model sketch from an initial Discovery Session

As you can see, the sketch contains Entities that were not mentioned such as Campaign Channel, Person and Team Member. These have been added as hypothetical Entities based upon the experience, for example that Teams are made up of People. These hypothetical additions will raise questions that need to be followed up, either within the session, or later.

Decide

So now we have held at least one planned session, it is time to take your discovery notes and think about turning them into data models!

What I always find is that as soon as I contemplate recording any of the discovery outcomes, I start to ask questions about *exactly* what it is that I *think* I have discovered.

---

70   Also see the RADM section in chapter 15.

Except for the very simplest data models, I have found that very little of the Real World immediately fits neatly into our data modelling syntax.

At each twist and turn of creating accurate data structures, decisions need to be made. This means that the information gleaned from the discovery sessions will almost inevitably give rise to further questions.

If possible, get immediate confirmation on minor points, either in the same sessions, or by a quick follow-up call or email. Whether you can adopt this approach will depend on the culture of the organisation and the relationships that you have established with the stakeholders in question. Some stakeholders will be fine with these informal approaches, others will not.

Often in the sessions though, there is so much to absorb that there is no time to think through all of the detail. It is only afterwards when you get a chance to do this that many additional questions come to light.

These new questions may need to feed into subsequent sessions that are already planned, or may give rise to further sessions being arranged. Hopefully, you may also be able to quickly resolve them using other follow-up interactions, such as emails, or quick calls.

Once the data models have been started, the task becomes a little more complicated, since now new discoveries may need to be cross checked against what has already been defined. Any discrepancies will raise yet more decisions that need to be made. Some of these will be to amend the definitions, others to feed more questions back into discovery activities.

To help think about the decision making activities, you may want to consider questioning in the following areas.

Degree of complexity

Whether the degree of complexity of a data model is appropriate is not always an easy question to answer. Sometimes the 'Do we care?' challenge will be required to determine whether a particular area or degree of complexity is actually worth representing in your model.

One thing to watch out for here is whether the complexity is as a result of overly complex Processes, or whether it is truly a reflection of how the corresponding Function would need to use data.

Another commonly encountered factor to consider in your decision is the stakeholder who provided the input! Some stakeholders love to over-complicate areas that after a lot of probing you find are really quite simple. Partly this may be because they focus on the minutiae without seeing any big picture pattern.

Also always remember that no matter how complex you make your model, it will *never* model the Real World *perfectly*. This means a line needs to be drawn somewhere.

So where do you draw this line of representation complexity?

When confronted by newly discovered complexity to represent in your data model, you should decide whether to:

1. Ignore it or

2. Simplify it or

3. Embrace a full representation of it

Each of these approaches has its own potentially undesirable outcomes. I'm afraid it will ultimately have to be your call. However, don't make it alone. Define and disseminate any conundrums and seek consensus on their resolution.

I also suggest that you evaluate the approaches in the order they are listed above. In other words only consider the second option *after* you decide that you definitely cannot ignore the newly discovered complexity!

Data availability scope

'Known and *Knowable'* represent two important characteristics of data's availability that may well need to be critically assessed when contemplating whether to include areas within your data models.

These terms provide challenges to the ease with which data can be made available to an organisation. The outcomes from these challenges can be used to judge the achievability of proposed benefits from requirements and also, importantly the definition of the boundary for the data model.

Let's look at exactly what is meant by these two terms.

Known

Data is all around us, some of it is *Known* and what we mean by this is that it is *recorded somewhere*, even if fleetingly.

That 'somewhere' is the interesting bit, for instance, the data may be known:

- in someone's head

- on a yellow sticky on someone's monitor

- in a shared spreadsheet

- in an organisation's Supply Chain Management (SCM) system

These examples illustrate the characteristics of data that pass the *Known* test, but the *Knowable* test applies further challenges to it.

Knowable

Even if data is *Known,* is it *Knowable?* What we mean by this is to challenge how *easily data can be made use of.* Typically, *Knowable* data implies that it is not isolated to the domain in which it is *Known.*

Therefore whether data is *Knowable* is an assessment of how easily it can use be made of.

Even if it is held in an organisation's SCM system, this is not necessarily the end of the *Knowable* challenge.

Do we care?

Possibly the most important question of Data Availability scope is that raised by the 'Do we care?' challenge.

If it is not feasible or desirable to source and track data reliably, then there may be no point in including its representation in your data model.

But unfortunately the response to this question may not be as simple as it might first appear.

Simply because data cannot currently be made available to the organisation, does not necessarily preclude it from being available at some point in the future. However, the counter argument to this is; what is the point in modelling it *now,* if it cannot possibly be sourced *now?* Why not wait until this sourcing *possibility* becomes a *reality?*

To help answer this question, it is worth asking 'What would be the *quantifiable benefit* of recording this data's definition and structure in the data model *now?*'

For example, when modelling Client Organisations, is it really of significance to track the ownership of one Organisation by one or more others? For organisations operating in Financial Markets, it may be critical to track such relationships. For other organisations, this data may be of absolutely no consequence to their operations, and therefore at best, simply 'Nice to know'.

Even if data would appear to be required, how realistic is it to be able to track it? This question invokes the Known and Knowable challenges. If the data cannot be tracked accurately, then it can quickly become stale. Once it starts to become stale, it can only offer negligible benefit because the reliability of any instance of it is questionable.

On the other hand, just because we can't create a realistic mechanism to track this data at the time of the data modelling effort, does not mean we will *never* be able to do so. For example, at some point in the near future we may be able to make use of a commercially available source such as a Web Service to constantly refresh this data into our organisation's systems.

A pragmatic approach to consider, is to create a placeholder structure with no more than a handful of Entities in it, but with very little in the way of Attribution. This structure can be represented on your data model to provide links to other structures in the model that are definitely within the current scope. But because it is not defined in detail, it won't squander precious effort.

Challenging Assumptions and Constraints

Many stakeholders are well able to provide you with a comprehensive list of constraints! You should consider such lists with a degree of scepticism and always make decisions as to their validity and impact.

Always try to think beyond the reported constraints to discover what their underlying *cause* is. This questioning may reveal that actually they are based solely upon the experience of the individual, rather than some universal law of the world.

In addition, you must be diligent and make constant critical assessments of any assumptions that *you* may have made in your model, even if unconsciously.

Key Point 87 *Removing constraints and challenging any assumptions driven by the 'now', yields a degree of resilience for an organisation leaving it better placed to face its un-knowable future.*

This is especially important for any scoping assumptions.

In my experience, constraints and assumptions are rarely immutable. Even though others have provided assertions that they <u>are</u> valid, you should always discover their origin in order to be satisfied that this is the case.
However, it may be wise to keep such scepticism to yourself until you have verified their validity or otherwise. Alienating yourself from stakeholders is a costly mistake that is not easy to remedy later!

Getting the data model 'correct'

Also, it is important to remember that there are no absolutes for a 'correct' data model. We need to accept the reality, which is that some data models will be closer to your organisation's Real World data meanings and patterns, than others. It is this reality that makes data modelling so challenging and, to my mind, so rewarding.

> **Key Point 88** **In reality there is not a single data model that <u>perfectly</u> represents your organisation's data meaning and patterns.**

To help you to check that your models are as close to ideal as possible, chapter 18 is devoted to the process of Quality Assuring them.

Define

In some ways creating the definitions in your data model is the simplest part of the entire Process, but at the same time keep in mind that the definition deliverables simply form the basis for sharing understanding.

In themselves, they are passive[71].

For more detail on the mechanics required to construct visual data models, please refer to the chapters in the Tools section of the book. What we will concentrate on in this chapter are the activities required in order to successfully define them.

Schedule Review Sessions

As your data models mature, you will need to start to organise Review Sessions. Some of these will be with stakeholders who provided input to your models in the first place. However, and somewhat weirdly, you may

---

71   Of course, never forget that Decisions need to be an integral part of the Defining activities.

actually learn more from those who were *not* involved in the initial Discover and Decide events.

This is because they will not have been subject to the decisions, assumptions and constraints that everyone else is familiar with, and will therefore see them with a fresh and critical eye.

During these sessions, the questioning style will be very different from the initial ones. By now there is a degree of confidence that the model provides an accurate representation of the Real World relevant to your organisation. This means that the questioning style will be much more 'Closed'.

Key Point 89   *The questioning style of Review Sessions will be more 'Closed' as you are really looking for confirmation of the model.*

This style is appropriate because you don't want to re-open a whole series of discussions that have already been resolved on the journey to get you to this stage.

But, at the same time, you should still listen carefully to ensure that there are no points being made that actually contradict the model. If there are, you must certainly explore them to convince yourself that the model does not require further work.

However, do not lose the focus of the sessions and it is of utmost importance that you avoid being diverted into 'covering old ground again'.

'Tweakening' data models

Data model *accuracy* is of course a phantom.

The trick is to recognise that you have reached the 'Good enough to go' level of its development. But how do you know when you have reached this point?

You may consider the following as tell-tale signs, when you are beginning to:

- tweak the model's micro structures repeatedly
- fiddle endlessly with datatype precisions
- wait repeatedly for feedback on clarifying a few more attribute's definitions with SMEs

If a couple of these sorts of signs characterise the current point in the modelling process, then consider either; having a break to come back to it afresh, or moving on to other activities that are more productive.

18: Quality Assuring Data Models

Introduction

From the first chapter onwards, this book has emphasised the important role that Logical Data Models play in defining, communicating and facilitating agreement on an organisation's data patterns and structures.

We are almost at the end of the data modelling process, but before we enter the Closure Process, it is time to verify the quality of the deliverables.

To assess the quality of data models, is to answer the question, 'How do we know for certain that our data models provide an *accurate* representation and can therefore yield the maximum possible benefit to the organisation?'

What this chapter describes, are the questions required and the definition of techniques that allow you to add a degree of objectivity to this evaluation. This objectivity will help you check and improve the quality of what you deliver and hence maximise its benefit.

The easier part of a data model's quality can be evaluated quite mechanically and this chapter includes a template that you can use to carry out such basic quality assurance of what is being delivered.

Although simple, in my experience these basic quality checks take a lot longer to carry out than you might expect. Therefore *before* you carry them out, you need to get the entire data model to the point that you are happy with the soundness of its structures and data patterns.

Data Model Completeness

To be effective, data models must represent our collective interpretation of the data in the Real World. If they do this, then we should be able to answer any hypothetical questions from them that we could ask of the Real World that they represent.

When we refer to quality assuring a data model, we are really trying to assess whether it is 'complete'.

But before we go any further, we must remind ourselves that realistically the data models will never be 'finished' and indeed will need to evolve in step with the organisation, even if the changes are minor.

Therefore what we mean by 'complete' means that we have defined it to the point where it satisfies the following demands:

- Adequate scope coverage

- Appropriate complexity

- Fully Normalised

Let's look at these three aspects in the following sections to discover how we can use an assessment of them to quality assure our data models.

Does the data model cover the required scope?

How do you know whether the entire required data scope of the data model is covered?

A few simple techniques that can be used to double check this are described below.

Functional support matrix

The first scoping test of your model should be carried as early as possible during the data modelling process, and therefore at a high level.

The quick way to do this, without getting bogged down into detailed analysis, is to use the Conceptual Data Model to produce a high level Function to Entity matrix. This can be used as a Tool to provide a sanity check to ensure appropriate coverage of any lower level models.

Finding a definition of the Functions may actually be the hard bit! If there is no defined list then you may need to collate one yourself. This can be based upon any Requirements documents that you may have access to, augmented by the findings from your Discovery Sessions.

Where this is particularly useful is for rapidly verifying very large and/or complex models. The simplified representation prevents the detail from getting in the way of the overall, high level, quality assurance of the model's completeness.

Testing Internal and External Entity boundaries

To ascertain whether a data model is complete, start to ask some hypothetical questions of the model at the *boundaries* of its scope. Figure 159 illustrates a very simple schematic of the Entity bounding.

What this diagram allows us to determine for any Entity on our data model, is whether it is defined Internally, Externally or is an Entity that provides links between these.

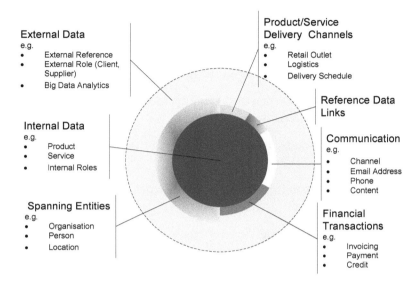

Figure 159 - Key Data Model Entity landscape

Okay so how can we use the illustration in figure 159 to check the completeness of our data models?

You should be able to position each Entity of your model clearly onto the data landscape of the diagram. Each should exist in one region only. If it is ambiguous which region an Entity is located within, then you need to look at its definition a little bit more closely.

The key Entities should link to other key Entities through the data structures of your models. For example, any Internally defined Entities such as Product definitions, should be located in the section in the middle. If however, the Products are being consumed in some way by a Client Entity, this would be located in the Outer zone.

The way that we track such consumption may involve Relationship pathways that pass through one or more Entities in other zones, such as; Logistics, Invoicing, Payments, Communication (Events).

Also remember that the Client Entity is actually an explicit Role played by an Organisation and so will need to be linked to their Organisation in the Spanning Entities zone.

This map allows you to probe the data structures that link the Entities. The answers should be provided by Relationship pathways between them.

Some examples of these are below:

- How does the Client get to know about the Product in the first place?

- How will payments be made and tracked against Order fulfilment?

- How is the Product delivered to the Client?

- Have we got the Person and Organisations linked appropriately to all of the above Entities?

- Is there only one pathway linking the Entities in the answer for each question?

    o If there is more than one pathway, what does each represent?

The main advantage to using this representation is that the layout of the Entities is reconfigured compared with the Logical Data Model. As a result, Entities are brought back into a single diagram that may have been dispersed across Subject Areas.

Figure 160 illustrates an example of the linking of the Entities via pathways that you can trace out on the diagram.

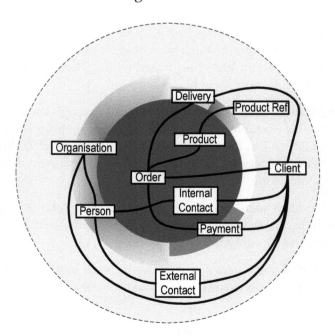

Figure 160 - Key Data Model Entity linkage example

Using this approach can be time consuming and so I suggest that you only record the *key* Entities on the schematic.

But in parallel, as you trace the pathways between them, you can cross reference and therefore verify these on your Logical Data Model. As you traverse the familiar data model to create the links, watch out for suspicious structures such as; Redundant Relationships and Fan Traps.

Temporal completeness

How will your model be affected by Time?

Almost every Entity on your model will be affected by Time to a degree.

A simple initial check will be to look for Entities that have no Date/Time Attributes and for each of these Entities you need to ask why there aren't any.

Although the data model has longevity, very little of today's data is immutable into the future. Even Reference Data has a degree of volatility that will need to be represented in your data models.

Recently working with a COTS product, a lot of work had been carried out to align the product workflows with the organisation's Processes. However, all of the workflow definitions assumed a 'steady state' Business as Usual (BAU) condition. If changes to the workflows were required, then the product supported this. But as soon as any changes were made, they would affect any workflows that were in-flight!

These kinds of temporal considerations need to be factored into your own data models. They will need to take into account that changes will inevitably occur mid-Lifecycle of at least some of the key Entities in your models.

This will determine that the Reference Data and any Meta Data will typically require Effective Date processing[72].

Lifecycle structures

A further set of challenges should be made to ensure that the data Lifecycles are adequately covered by the model. Here checks should be made to ensure that the data structures for each relevant Entity, support the data patterns that need to be captured over time.

Lifecycle modelling will involve one or more of the following model patterns:

- Start and End Date processing

---

72   See chapter 14 for more detail on this.

- State tracking
- Status Transition
- Milestone attainment
- Phase tracking
- Versioning

Where your model features Lifecycle data behaviour, look at your data structures to ensure that they are appropriate. Cross reference them with the Tools that we learned in chapter 14 to make sure that there are no variations that you cannot explain.

Is it Future-proofed?

In chapter 3 we looked at how, if sufficiently accurate, data models can have longevity measured in decades. Another way of challenging the model's completeness is to look at how it would accommodate future deviations from the present.

But how do we do this?

A simple question to ask in all Subject Areas is; 'Are the structures sufficiently flexible to provide extensible future-proofing?'

Spend some time revisiting the Extensible data structures illustrated in chapter 13. Make sure that you have incorporated extensible structures in areas of your model that you suspect will be subject to volatility of *data* definitions.

Obviously, if defining Global data models, you will as a standard approach need to use Extensible structures across most of the key definition Entities of your organisation's operational data.

Remove Mechanistic references

In chapter 1, we described the importance of removing mechanisms from our definitions. Carry out a simple check of any mechanistic aspects of a data model's definitions. Where they do exist then make any corresponding corrections to it. This will assist in making its temporal definition more long lived and therefore 'complete'.

Review constraints

Constraints are rarely immutable in my experience. Review any constraints that you have recorded to see whether they are truly the result of some inalienable law of the universe, or may actually be swept aside at some point in the future.

The harder constraints to challenge are the ones that have snuck in without notice. When assessing an Entities description, instead of asking 'Is this correct?', change the tense of the question to 'Will this *always be* correct?' This will hopefully uncover the unconscious constraints that have been baked into the data model.

Standard Operating Models

Where Standard Operating Models (SOMs) have been defined by your organisation, they can provide very useful feedback to Quality Assure your data models.

SOMs should define data usage by the defined Processes. These can therefore be used at a lower level than the Functional Support Matrix that we covered earlier to check the scope of the data models.

If part of the data usage is not covered by the data models, then you need to decide whether the data should be considered in scope, out of scope, or possibly irrelevant or incorrect.

Similarly, if there are areas of the data model that are not covered by the SOM definitions, then you need to get to the bottom of why this is so.

Check reporting requirements

To provide an additional cross reference for your scoping validation, it can pay dividends to look at reporting, or other documented requirements. For each of these data requirements, you need to check that the necessary supporting data structures exist.

Don't forget though, that any *specified* requirements should be used as *clues* to the *full set* of potential data requirements. So, in other words, the reporting data scope should be less than or equal to the data model scope.

Group review to validate

Checking a data model for its completeness is a very difficult activity. In my experience, the best way to validate a data model is to review it with other people.

Admittedly, it is not always easy to find people that you can review the data model with that have sufficient:

- skills
- knowledge
- time
- inclination

However, if you can review your data model with others, then the process of walking them through it will also test *your* understanding, as much as whether the participants actually agree with what the data model conveys.

Reverse engineering

You may also want to consider Reverse Engineering an existing Physical Data Model, to sanity check 'Have we thought of everything or is there anything we've missed?' style interrogations of your models.

A word of warning though; there is a perception that Logical Data Models can simply be constructed from earlier models and/or data interface specifications, in other words, using a Reverse Engineering approach. Whilst this has some merit, extreme caution should be exercised with this technique.

Key Point 90   *Blindly Reverse Engineering system definitions to form the basis of new Logical Data Models, runs a significant risk of constraining an organisation's <u>future</u> to the <u>mistakes</u> of its <u>past</u>!*

Wholesome Structures

So the scope is assured but we also need to validate the structures represented in our data models. This section is devoted to describe challenges to it that will uncover any deficiencies in this.

Is the model sufficiently detailed?

To assess whether the data model structures are sufficiently complex we can make use of a principle nicely encapsulated by the Albert Einstein quote:

'A scientific theory should be as simple as possible, but no simpler.'

Let's appropriate this quote, for a way of looking at the process of data modelling.

Key Point 91   *Data models should be as simple as possible, but no simpler.*

The graphic in Figure 161 illustrates this idea.

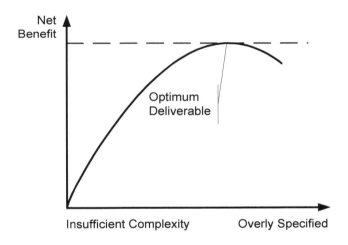

Figure 161 - Optimum data model

Determining where your model sits on the trajectory illustrated in figure 161 is not always easy.

There is a careful balance here between; the modelling process having longevity and accuracy that allows its benefit to be maximised, but is not overly complex.

This judgement is a fine one and is one that, although never easy, does get easier with experience. To assist with this judgement and to try to make it slightly more objective use the technique in the following section.

Too wide/insufficient depth (insufficient Normalisation)

A key benefit from adopting a methodical layout to your models is that the models become easier and quicker to Quality Assure. One of the most difficult aspects to review in a data model is the appropriateness of the level of detail it holds.

How do you know that it is sufficiently detailed and that is has been fully Normalised?

Just glance *momentarily* at figure 162.

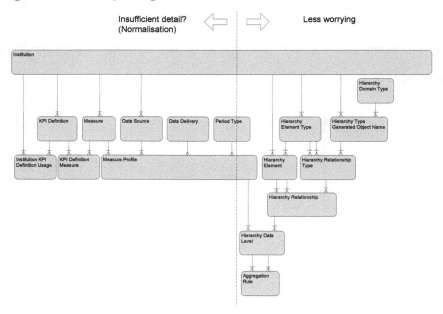

Figure 162 – Data Model has lack of depth for its width

Without concentrating on the detail of the Entities in figure 162, I hope that something immediately strikes you about this model fragment. What I have noticed over the years is that the ratio of width to depth is an indicator of 'wholesomeness'. It shouldn't be too wide for its depth nor too deep for its width.

Obviously this is not *true*; there is no range of aspect ratios that a 'good' data model must fall within.

However, notice on the left hand side that the structure is a lot wider than it is deep. Immediately this would draw my attention as an area that needs to be prioritised for Quality Assurance review.

This characteristic does not *necessarily* make it wrong, but it would make me want to probe this side of the model with more zeal than the right hand side.

What I would set about doing is to examine the patterns and structures to see if they require more complexity, by further decomposition or Normalisation.

This quick check has always yielded benefit, but the next section looks at more methodical way to validate sufficient Normalisation.

Normalisation

We learned that there are two key data modelling clues that reveal insufficient Normalisation in our data models:

1. Repeated Values for Attributes – new Master Entity

2. Repeated single Attributes, or groups of Attributes – new Detail Entity

To ensure that the data model has sufficient level of complexity in terms of its Normalisation we should look for these two aspects in the definitions of our data models.

The process of Normalisation is an important technique that must be employed when evolving Logical Normalised Data Models to 'completion' from their Conceptual antecedents.

However, many data models contain Attributes that are sneaky De-normalisations. Look critically at your model to ensure that this has not inadvertently happened in your modelling endeavours.

The Status of an Entity may well be something of interest for an organisation, but the inclusion of an Attribute to record this actually disguises the fact that a data structure is missing from the model.

As another example, an Attribute named Order Status is typically really the Order *Current* Status. This makes it clear that it is the De-normalised Status and indicates that a structure is required to record the Status Lifecycle.

Repeated values for Attributes

There are three possible sources that you can check to see whether the data will have repeated values that indicate further Normalisation needs to take place:

1. Attribute definitions in your data models – particularly the list of example values

2. Data samples that stakeholders provided - such as spreadsheets or similar

3. Attribute names – look for parts of the name that indicate a typing or grouping or another Entity

Although laborious, combing through the Attributes should uncover any of these that need to be fully Normalised.

Repeated single or groups of Attributes

Where you see repeating Attributes or repeating groups of Attributes, this indicates that a Detail Entity is required. Often the qualification of the Attribute gives away that it needs to be reviewed.

In the Syntax section we looked at two examples of this symptom:

1. Single Attributes – Allocation Date, Site Attendance Date, Completion Date

2. Attribute Groups – **Registered** Address XXX, **Postal** Address XXX, **Contact** Address XXX

Rule Based Modelling structures

Rule Based Modelling technique is all about modelling data rules that can prescribe Lifecycles, Business and Data Rules and Data Behaviours. Let's examine these again from a Quality Assurance perspective.

We saw in chapter 13 that there is a principle of Reflection arising from Rule Based Modelling. This principle specifies that; if there are data rules about Entity Relationships at a specific level, then these should almost certainly be reflected at the level of abstraction above and/or below it.

By laying your models out as suggested in chapter 6, any Rule Based Modelling patterns are revealed and any symmetry, or lack of it, is immediately made clear. Thus any potential anomalies can be easily identified.

So how about the model fragment illustrated in figure 163?

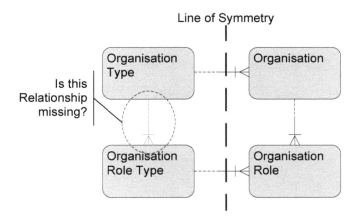

Figure 163 – Quality Assuring model Reflections – missing Relationship?

In this model fragment, we notice a vertical line of symmetry between the Types and their corresponding Entities that are related to each other. However, there is no Relationship between the Type Entities that is a reflection of the one between the instance Entities.

This immediately raises the question why not?

The principle of Reflection is a powerful Tool that helps us to spot such anomalies in our models. Unfortunately there is no stock answer as to whether the anomalies uncovered are right or wrong! You will have to examine them and ensure that they make sense.

Fan Traps

In chapter 10 we learned about Fan Traps, which are patterns that, if mentioned at all, are painted as villainous patterns that always need to be eradicated. However, the pattern is not *inherently* a bad structure. As with any Tool, it may be used inappropriately, but when used correctly, provides a very powerful modelling technique.

So what are we looking for when Quality Assuring the use of Fan Traps in our data models?

Firstly let's remind ourselves of the pattern and its use as in figure 164.

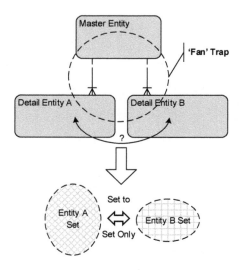

Figure 164 – Fan Traps – good or bad?

Fan Traps allow the data model to represent the interrelationship of two *sets* of data representing different things. A Fan Trap is an appropriate model where what is required is a:

- set to set comparison or

- the set related to a single instance

An example of an area to look at, was contained in figure 145. This has been highlighted to reveal the Fan Traps in figure 165.

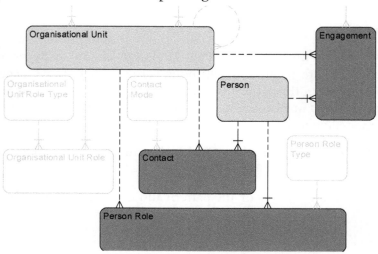

Figure 165 – Spotting Fan Traps in data models

Notice that there are three Fan Traps involving the Person Entity.

If we ever want to know a relationship between a single instance of one of the Detail Entities to a single instance of another Detail Entity then this would make it an incorrect Tool to use. For example, we cannot relate a single Engagement instance, to a specific Contact instance.

This model may not necessarily be wrong but by identifying the Fan Traps quickly we can probe whether it is correct.

The Basic Quality Assurance Check List

Once you are happy with the scope, the data structures and patterns in your model, it is time to systematically check at a detailed level, every element that it contains!

Be warned though, that this basic Quality Assuring of the model is a *very* time consuming task.

Listed here are a set of basic checks that you should consider applying.

Area	Feature	Check?
Data Model Subject Area	Legend	Every Subject Area has got the basic context information recorded.
	Shared Entities	It contains at least one Entity that is shared with another Subject Area.
Entity	Name	1. Concise and meaningful 2. No Plurals 3. No Acronyms 4. No current Process or Mechanisms baked in 5. Synonyms included

Area	Feature	Check?

Entity	**Unique Identifier**	1. Sufficient Mandatory and Stable Attributes
		
		2. Surrogates *only* where Entity is *Internally defined*
		
		3. Any External Mastering is by stable authorisation bodies
		
		4. *Minimum* UID components are:
		
		   a. One Attribute
		
		   b. Two or more Identifying Relationships
		
		   c. One Identifying Relationship *and* one Attribute
		
		5. Date included where Entity can resurrect

	Description	1. Concise and meaningful to all stakeholders 2. Contains examples
	Data Rules	Not too prescriptive, but prescriptive where basic rules *cannot change* e.g. 'End Date is not defined or >= Start Date.'
	Business Rules	Defined with meaningful examples. Often these require the definition of Roles – are these defined in the model and correctly related?
	Lifecycle definition	How, when and by whom does an instance get created, modified and deprecated.

Area	Feature	Check?
Super-type and Sub-types	**Validity**	1. Physically different in the Real World 2. Attributes different 3. Operationally treated similarly 4. Similar core Relationships
Attributes	**Name**	1. Concise and meaningful 2. No Plurals 3. No Acronyms 4. No current Process or Mechanisms baked in 5. Synonyms included
	Meta Data	1. Optionality defined 2. Datatype defined 3. Size is *qualified* (i.e. Small, Medium or Large)
	Description	1. Concise and meaningful to all stakeholders 2. Contains examples
	Properties	1. Atomic 2. Non-dependent 3. Stable 4. Knowable (Staleness test) 5. Is it Boolean or does it reference a Domain? 6. Visibility rules are defined 7. Capture and maintenance rules are defined

Area	Feature	Check?
Relationships	Name	1. Concise and meaningful 2. No Plurals 3. No Acronyms 4. No current Process or Mechanisms baked in 5. Synonyms included
	Cardinality	1. No M:M Relationships allowed 2. No 1:1 Relationships allowed 3. Check if Non-Transferrable
	Optionality	Check whether Mandatory Relationships should be Optional and Optional Relationships should be Mandatory.
	Recursive Relationships	All M:M Relationships resolved using: 1. Standard Intersection Entity pattern or 2. Grouping pattern?
	Redundant paths Organisation Organisational Unit Employee	If there is more than one way two Entities are related, check to see if one or more of them are redundant.

19: Closure Processes

Introduction

The Closure Processes signal the end game of the 3-D Modelling Process and therefore need to be delivery and consumer focussed.

If your organisation already has either; a Data Governance Framework, or Master Data Management framework, then these should define processes that prescribe the dissemination and communication mechanisms for your deliverables.

However, unless there is absolutely no time available, do not consider that this will be the limit of the dissemination effort.

The data model definitions must have a transformational impact on the organisation. This means that simply storing them in model repositories that no-one has access to, will effectively thwart any possible benefits that they otherwise could deliver.

Of course, in the absence of any existing frameworks, it will be up to you to determine what happens with your deliverables. They should have a positive impact, but how this is achieved will require a degree of thought.

Either way, the activities that you should consider as part of the Closure Processes are described in this chapter.

Model Dissemination

Whatever you do with the deliverables from the data modelling effort, do not leave them abandoned in some forgotten backwater where they will effectively 'disappear'.

My preference is to make my data models accessible to 'everyone', so Wiki or Document Management environments are good repositories for this purpose. Increasingly software tools are able to fulfil data model dissemination requirements, so it is definitely worth taking some time to research what is available.

Converting the data models into consumer-friendly lightweight formats, such as XPS or PDFs, can also provide widespread accessibility. This allows anyone to consume the data structure definitions without requiring them to have access to the modelling tool in which they are recorded.

However, remember that these files need to be kept current, and so I suggest that they are created only once the data models are 'complete' or at least beyond the 'Good enough to go' stage. Remember though, that unless these are under the control of a Data Governance Framework, they will likely become stale, as no-one will be tasked with keeping them current.

Also, remember that the visual data model structures are only part of the data model definitions and so you will need to specify how the remaining definitions will be shared.

Accessible model repository

An effective dissemination mechanism for your data model is to provide a comprehensive Knowledgebase. This needs to be widely accessible across the organisation and provide multiple communication styles.

For example, consider using a WikiMedia Wiki. This can deliver data model definitions including:

- Descriptive articles

- Data Model image files

- Data Lexicon

- Integration with other Intranet and Internet based resources

A major benefit of a Wiki is that it encourages shared ownership through shared authorship.

In chapter 1 we mentioned that one difficulty with SMEs is their availability to provide specialist input. By providing a Wiki as a channel for recording their expertise we can help reduce the pressure on their time to the overall benefit of the organisation.

I have seen this approach work very successfully for a number of different organisations, but its success does rely on Wiki enthusiasts championing this way of working in the early stages.

Objections to a Wiki are typically:

1. No-one has the time to create Wiki articles (especially hard pressed SME's!)

2. Wiki-like knowledge repositories already exist

3. Concern about leakage of competitive IP by making it 'public'

4. Concern over Governance and control of content

These are very real considerations and would need to be addressed by any proposal to use a Wiki.

Provide Knowledge Transfer Sessions

I am sure that by now you will have noticed a preference on my part for active sessions. You will guess therefore that sending an email to a group of stakeholders with a data model attached is probably not my preferred dissemination mechanism. If possible, I hold active briefing sessions to take people through what is being delivered and provide them with a summary of the impacts to their worlds.

Try to target key stakeholders, such as:

- Project Managers, Product Owners

- Transformation/Programme Managers

- CDOs, CIOs, CTOs

- Design Authority stakeholders

- the Enterprise Architecture community

These stakeholders need to promote what you are developing to ensure that it will have a real impact across the organisation. Therefore, you will need their confidence and buy-in with what you have produced. This is especially true where the models will be used within the context of any system development or deployment.

A word of warning; these key stakeholders will need to have been brought on the journey, as a fundamental disagreement with your final deliverables will be catastrophic!

Liaise With Consumers

If you have not managed to identify any direct consumers of your deliverables, then you need to consider that there really *should be* some. This may cause you to identify and engage with stakeholders as *candidate* consumers.

I remember developing a Global Data Model (GDM) for one Client. Although there were no signed-up consumers for the deliverables, there were certainly plenty of projects that immediately required the GDM as the basis for their work.

As a team, we did not simply complete the GDM, socialise a link to the models and then move on to other projects. We forged positive ongoing engagements that meant the GDM became an accepted part of the development and delivery processes across the organisation. In parallel with our GDM development, we sought out Product Owners and established contact. Briefing sessions were then held to explain the benefits that GDM adoption would bring, both to their Work-streams and to the wider organisation.

This evangelising is so important!

We hadn't undertaken this approach for very long before it gained its own momentum and additional Product Owners and Programme Managers as well as Architects started to contact us asking how they could make use of the GDM.

Creating a User Guide

Don't forget that you will become the SME for the data models that you develop!

The consequence of this will be an ongoing commitment for you with respect to the models. This will be the case, whether or not the organisation recognises it. This commitment will require you to act as the liaison point for the deliverables going forward.

To help mitigate the effort required for this role, you should consider creating one or more Artifacts that explain the way that the data model can be used by consumers.

This should include the following elements:

1. Data model Key SME list

2. Data model adoption Benefits

3. Engagement model

These elements are described in the following sections.

Data model Key SME list

A list of the key stakeholders who were involved in the data modelling exercise needs to be recorded, so that consumers know who they can contact about the data models.

Typically the data model will have longevity that is far greater than the employment of the stakeholders whose input led to its definitions. Even you may well move on before the data models cease to be relevant. So especially for those who come after, this list will give them a starting point of people to contact who are still within the organisation.

Data model adoption benefits

This section of the User Guide will identify the tangible benefits delivered by adopting the data models.

They will typically include:

- Reduced effort and costs

- Reduced risks (not creating novel data models)

- Improved development quality (proven patterns of deliverables already exist)

- Improved conformance with Enterprise definitions

- Removal of silos of data since data exchange is simplified (Apples are Apples in all systems)

Engagement model

The Engagement Model for the data model adoption needs to describe how the data models are integrated with the consumers own processes. Typically this means some degree of formality around the liaison between the consumers and the data model custodians.

This may already be prescribed by a framework such as a Data Governance Framework or may be less formal.

However, one of the key elements in this will be to define how changes identified during this engagement may be fed back to become part of the ongoing definition of the data model. Also how changes are propagated out to any existing or in-flight deployments should be described.

A simple data model Consumer Engagement Model that you may want to use as a starting point for your own for is shown in figure 166.

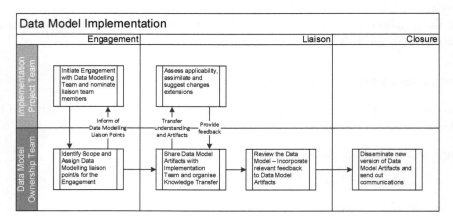

Figure 166 - Data Model Engagement template

Integration With Data Governance Processes

If there are Data Governance Processes and/or Master Data Management Processes that are already documented then you will need to research these and work out how you need to integrate your activities with them.

Ideally at the very least, the Enterprise Logical Data Model will form a cornerstone in any such frameworks. If not, it might be worth expending some effort to ensure that it does become an integral part of the frameworks. This is because it is difficult to see how these frameworks can be truly effective without being based upon the shared and agreed understanding of the data!

Hopefully any framework processes will be lightweight and simple, so that integrating with them is not onerous. If this is the case, then it should make your job easier as there will be dissemination mechanisms already specified, and links already created to the relevant stakeholders.

20: What Happens Next?
Physical Data Models

Introduction

A repeating theme of this book is the importance of bringing benefit to your organisation through data model definitions. They can only achieve this if they allow it to operate in a way that was previously denied to it.

So far on our journey of discovery, we have learned about the Tools and activities required to define an organisation's data models. But, if they become buried in a repository somewhere that no-one ever looks at, how can they possibly have any impact and therefore what has been the point of all that work?

The Logical Data Model needs to be a key part of the organisation's effective operational basis and therefore must become a pillar in the wider family of Enterprise Data Models.

Collectively these models can deliver an enormously positive impact on an organisation's data, by establishing the foundations for its shared understanding of its data.

Their primary importance is to provide a framework by which the organisation, its stakeholders and its implemented systems, can be better aligned.

This chapter considers the types of data models and associated Artifacts that should be thought of as Enterprise Data Models. It also examines each one's purpose and thus what they need to define and communicate.

Although not intended to be provide a comprehensive transformation design guide, this chapter also describes the way that the Logical Data Models can be transformed into Physical Data Models.

The Enterprise Data Models' Composition

In chapter 1 we discovered that data models define the structure and patterns that are required to support an organisation's operations. Arguably they should be fundamental to enhancing an organisation's success.

The Conceptual and Logical Data Models cannot do this on their own. They need to be augmented by a more comprehensive set of definitions to have a significant impact.

This family of related models is called the Enterprise Data Models. In this chapter we will discover what this family of data models comprise, and how they are related to the Conceptual and Logical Data Models.

The Enterprise Data Models include the following:

- Conceptual Data Models

- Logical Data Models

- Physical Data Models

- Canonical Models

Benefits from Enterprise Data Models

In the first chapter, we discovered that to maximise the benefit from data for an organisation, we need to agree the meaning of the data across the organisation. Enterprise Data Models provide the comprehensive foundation for this *agreed data meaning across* an organisation.

> **Key Point 92**   *All Enterprise Data Models must be based upon the firm foundations of the organisation's <u>shared and agreed understanding of its data</u>.*

Significant organisational gains can be realised from using Enterprise Data Models as the basis for any data related changes, including improvements in the following:

1. Convergence

2. Conformance

3. Coherence

4. Agility gains

5. Risk reduction

The way that these can be achieved is described in more detail in the book 'Enterprise Data Architecture: How to navigate its landscape' by the same author.

Data Model Inter-Relationships

The Enterprise Data Models are not independent of each other; at their very core they are absolutely dependent on shared definitions of data meanings and data patterns.

The underlying basis for all of them should be the Conceptual Data Model.

It is this basic model that should be the solid foundational base on which the Logical Data Models are constructed. These models take the high level definitions of the organisation's data and create more detailed and Normalised Data Models from it.

Once the Logical Data Models are agreed, an organisation will have the firm basis for the defined data requirements of its operations.

Figure 167 illustrates the relationships between the various Enterprise Data Models. They span a range of abstraction; the most abstract are the Conceptual Data Models and the most specific are those models that are to do with individual Physical Data Model implementations.

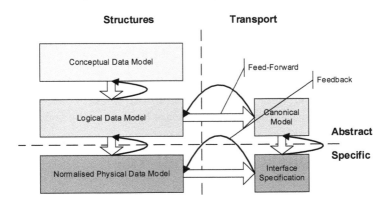

Figure 167 - Enterprise Data Model Inter-relationships

Feed forward and feedback processes

To have an impact on an organisation, the Enterprise Data Models need to be *all pervasive* and this is, of course, crucial for any IT system related activities. When used within this context, formal engagement processes need to be defined for the adoption of the Enterprise Data Models.

Obviously to be influential, the models' definitions need to feed forward into any implementation processes. However, a key part of the engagement process definitions, should also be processes where any feedback is also evaluated.

Any *appropriate* changes from the more specific implementations should be incorporated into the more abstracted levels. This can arise, for example, where more detailed understanding in particular areas may be uncovered, or new data sources may become available and consumed by the organisation.

> **Key Point 93**   *Only modifications that are truly of significance within more abstracted models should be made from discoveries at more specific levels.*

As an example, consider a new Attribute that is defined due to a specific implementation. If this Attribute is assessed to have an Enterprise wide significance then it would need to be added to the Enterprise Logical Data Model.

The feedback loops reinforce the idea that the models will never be *finished* or *static*, but will always have a limited degree of *fluidity*.

Of course, the feed forward and any feedback mechanisms, should be a part of any overall Data Governance Framework and/or Master Data Management process definitions.

The Conceptual Data Models and Logical Data Models have already been covered in depth in chapter 15. We will therefore concentrate on defining the other models comprising the Enterprise Data Models in the following sections.

Enterprise Implementation Patterns

If we have recorded the definitions of the data patterns and structures accurately in our Enterprise Data Models, then they can form a coherent basis for Enterprise Design Patterns. These Enterprise Design Patterns can then be used to bring concrete transformation benefits to implementations in the system landscape as illustrated in figure 168.

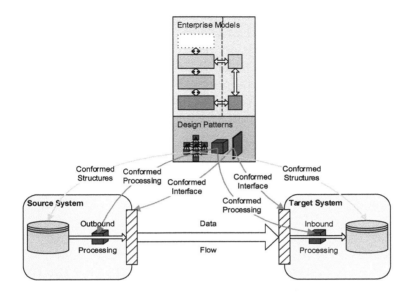

Figure 168 – Using Enterprise Data Models to drive delivery

What this will allow us to achieve is to conform the definitions and structures of our data into the system landscape and at the same time, boost the organisation's ability to respond rapidly to change.

This is an extremely potent tool for aligning, streamlining and creating true system agility for the organisation!

Moreover, this approach will ensure that the data's meaning will be conformed in all technologies. This must remain true, whether we consider either Data at Rest or Data in Flow. This requirement is illustrated conceptually in figure 169.

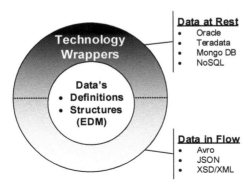

Figure 169 – Conforming the meaning of our data across the system landscape

What this figure makes clear, is that the definitions and structures of our data must remain constant, no matter what constraints the technologies impose on us. For example, there will certainly be different technology constraints for Oracle compared with Mongo DB, or XSDs versus Avro. But these differences should not cause any deviations from our data's definitions and structures. Through this approach, we can retain the data's essence; the precious meaning that you have distilled and enshrined in the data models!

Be careful here though! Many Technologists and implementation folk will state that because we are using a non-Relational Database or self-describing data payloads, we can simply ignore the Logical Data Models.

But we cannot.

Key Point 94 *The definitions, Relationships and any data rules that we have defined in our Logical Data Models must still hold true irrespective of any implementation constraints.*

Obviously, our Logical Data Models are easier to implement in a 3NF Relational Database, but the models should have been defined from the Business and/or Operational understanding of our data. This understanding is key and must not be lost in an implementation. If it is, we face the high probability that the implementation's data cannot be shared across the organisation.

Even de-normalised implementations should respect our Logical Data Models and we'll look at the rules that constrain the de-normalised structures and meanings later in this chapter.

Data at Rest - Physical Data Models

The following sections list some of the headline transformations that take place if making the transition from a Logical Data Model to a Relational Physical Data Model. Even in the Big Data era, we may well represent our data through a normalised Hive SQL layer and so the following patterns are still relevant.

Resolving Keys

When making the transition from a Logical Data Model to a normalised Relational Database Data Model, some basic transformations are required for the Unique Identifiers and Relationships.

This section illustrates the simple direct transformation patterns.

Primary Keys

Without any designed transformations, each Unique Identifier that is defined in the Logical Data Model, using one or more Attributes, would create one or more corresponding Columns in the Primary Key of a Table, as illustrated in figure 170.

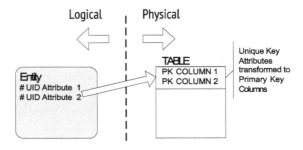

Figure 170 – Unique Identifier to Primary Key direct transformation

Typically Database designers and developers favour Integer ID columns to represent the Primary Key of the Tables. As a result, if you have not used Numeric Surrogate Keys for the Unique Identifiers in the Logical Data Model, then the Primary Keys will deviate from the Logical Data Model Unique Identifier Attributes.

This scenario is illustrated in figure 171.

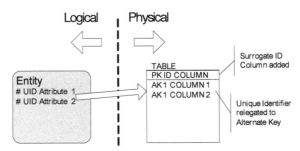

Figure 171 – Unique Identifier to Primary Key, a more typical transformation

In this case it is important to retain the understanding of your Unique Identifiers and record them as an Alternate Keys or Unique Keys within the Physical Data Model.

These can then be used to:

- Enforce the Uniqueness in the manner that the Logical Data Model specifies

- Inform stakeholders who need to identify each instance for:

  o ETL Processing

  o Data Quality duplicate checking

Foreign Keys

Foreign Keys are the physical equivalents of the Relationships in our Logical Data Models[73]. For each column of the Primary Key of the Master Table, a Foreign Key Column is added to the Detail Table.

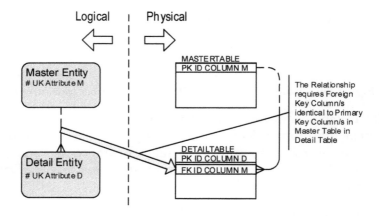

Figure 172 – Relationship to Foreign Key transformation

Foreign Keys as Primary Keys

Where the Relationships are Identifying Relationships in the Logical Data Model, then a simple transformation would make the Primary Key of the Detail Table include the Foreign Key Column/s.

This is illustrated in figure 173.

---

73 Many data modelling tools already represent Relationships using Foreign Key Attributes in the Logical Data Model.

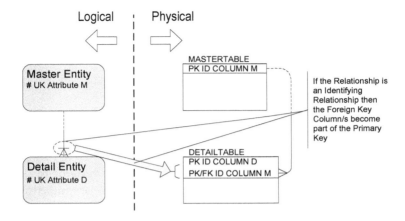

Figure 173 – Identifying Relationship to Foreign Key + Primary Key

Chained Identifying Relationships

Where the Identifying Relationships are cascaded down through the Entities in the Logical Data Model, this results in the Foreign Keys also cascading down through the Physical Data Model. This would result in the Primary Keys adding more Columns as it gets passed from Master to Detail and in turn to its Detail and so on.

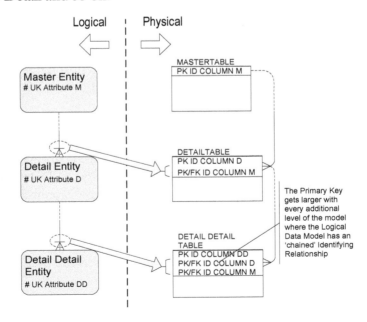

Figure 174 – Chained Unique Identifiers

Often for this reason, designers like to break the chaining of the Primary Key using Surrogate Primary Keys. But this approach also has its own design impacts that need to be considered. In actual fact, there are some advantages to retaining the cascading Keys to the lowest levels.

Data in Flow – Interface Models

In the Introduction to the book, we saw that data models are more important than ever, but that their role has radically changed in the last decade. Increasingly, the challenges that organisations face are not caused by custom development, but instead, arise from the requirement to plug Cloud based solutions together to form the backbone of the organisation's system landscape. As a result, the Data at Rest definitions are not nearly as important as those of Data in Flow.

> *Key Point 95*   *Enterprise Data at Rest definitions are of diminishing importance within this new data era, and conversely Data in Flow definitions have become absolutely critical to prevent us from creating data silos and also to boost the organisation's 'system agility'.*

It is essential to get this approach right in a loosely coupled world. But surely, although our data models are good at describing physical data structures, we won't be able to use them to define our interface definitions?

Well, in fact we can and we should.

The Data at Rest usage of our models has become increasingly marginalised, relegated to the relatively rare implementations of Operational Data Stores or other aggregation hubs, such as Hadoop Clusters, or Data Warehouses. However, everywhere that our data flows across the organisation's system landscape, the Logical Data Models must hold sway. We must always be vigilant though; our interface definitions must not be based upon any physical transformations. This is because these definitions will have been modified by design processes and will often have compromised the definitions of the Logical Data Models.

> **Key Point 96** *The Logical Data Models must be used to conform the Data in Flow definitions to ensure optimal flows of data across our organisation's system landscape.*

In fact, they have become the crucial foundation of data's definitions and structures for the interfaces in a loosely coupled system landscape. The data exchanges in today's system landscapes are predominated by format frameworks like XSDs and JSON/Avro.

> **Key Point 97** *High Level Interface Models must be formed using the Logical Data Models as their basis.*

Figure 175 shows an example of using the Logical Data Models to rigorously define interface definitions. These need to be defined at a level that is abstracted above individual implementations, and must be used to conform the individual 'protocols' for the Data in Flow mechanisms e.g. XSDs.

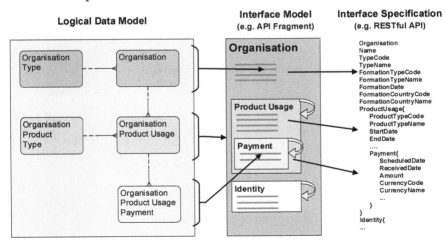

Figure 175 – Logical Data Model conformance for Interface definitions

The example in figure 175, shows the principle of creating a definition that acts above the individual API definitions. Notice that it clearly shows how we can determine the definitions and structures of the data in the interfaces, from the definitions and structures of the Logical Data Model.

The APIs may be defined multiple times across the system landscape, but each needs to have conformance with an authority for their definition that is created at a higher level. This will allow them to be created using a 'pick n mix' approach from the higher level definitions, but by inheriting their definitions and structures we will guarantee consistency and interoperability across individual implementations. And, of course, this mastering of meaning needs to be adopted across the different Interface mechanisms such as within JSON/Avro formats.

As a result of using this approach, we can ensure that all our interfaces will 'play nicely together'.

De-Normalised Physical Models

Consider the circle of development of data models and data flows that is represented in Figure 176.

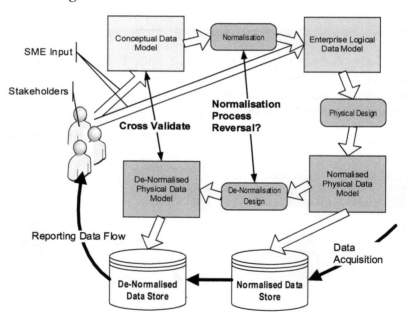

Figure 176 - De-normalising the Normalised models

This schematic suggests that the De-normalised models can be considered as providing at least a partial reversal of the Normalisation processes that produced the Normalised Logical and Physical Data Models.

In this respect, the data sourced from the implemented De-normalised data structures via reporting, is effectively brought back to stakeholders with a representation that is familiar to them. It was (hopefully) this exact same stakeholder understanding that formed the basis of the Conceptual and Normalised Logical Data Models in the first place.

Comparing the De-normalised and Conceptual Models may well be a fruitful exercise for the Data Modeller as it may drive changes to either or both models, based upon the definitions held in the other.

De-normalised Physical Data Models

The design decisions for De-normalising a highly Normalised Model may be complex and arise for many reasons including reporting needs or performance gains.

However, when considering De-normalised Models, some people immediately think of Dimensional models and possibly also standard Star or Snowflake Schema Dimensional modelling styles, as if these are the only structures that could be used.

Key Point 98 **De-normalised Models need to represent data in a way that fits an <u>organisation's needs</u>.**

Whilst useful, styles specified by Data Warehousing modelling luminaries should only be used as sanity checks for models that the Data Modeller evolves.
An organisation's needs may not necessarily be best served by slavish adoption of models that can be found in books or on the internet!

When evolving these models, their relationship to the Conceptual and High Level Logical Models cannot be ignored.

Typical De-Normalisation approaches

De-normalised Data Models typically have a pre-eminent requirement to simplify the access to the data for reporting purposes. This means that removing joins from queries is an important factor. Essentially this is achieved by flattening the structures.

In chapter 8 we looked at the Normalisation process and spotted two general patterns that this process delivers. In the same way, we can consider that the reverse patterns apply when designing De-normalised Data Models.

Flattening Master Entities

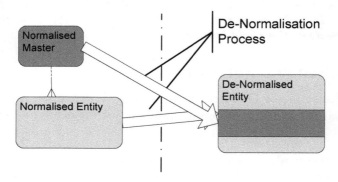

Figure 177 – De-normalising Master Entities

So if we reverse the Normalisation process that led to us creating the Registration Authority as a separate Entity, we get the resulting data model fragment as in figure 178.

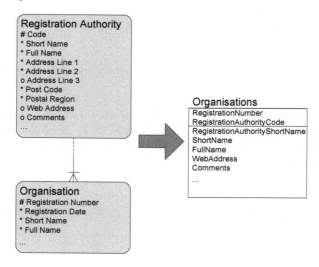

Figure 178 – De-normalising Master Entities

What about where we have a structure in the Master Entity such as a hierarchy?

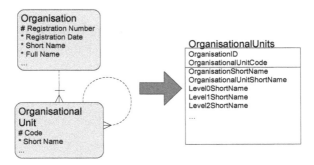

Figure 179 – De-normalising Hierarchies

Figure 179 illustrates a simplified flattening of this into a typical De-normalised representation. Notice how the hierarchy levels have been flattened into the highest Level0 to the lowest – Level2. We can see immediately that we are constraining the number of Levels and their naming into the data structures. As a result we are compromising their flexibility and future-proofed qualities. But the design trade-off here, is the presentation of the data without the consumer needing to figure out how to traverse the Hierarchy from the Normalised structures.

Flattening Detail Entities

Where we had repeating single Attributes, or repeating groups of Attributes, these informed us that we needed to Normalise an additional Detail Entity in the Logical Data Models.

Again there is a standard pattern that can be used to reverse this technique and De-normalise these Entities back into the Master Entity's physical representation.

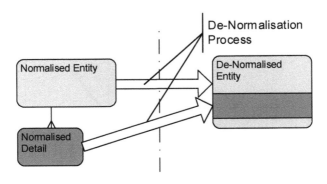

Figure 180 – De-normalising Detail Entities

Qualified Instance Detail Entity data

One general case of flattening Detail Entity data is where there can only be one guaranteed instance of the Detail per Master instance. For example, we can imagine that each Organisation can have multiple Addresses, but that there is only one that is the 'Registered Address'. Figure 181 illustrates how we can flatten the qualified instances into the Master Entity.

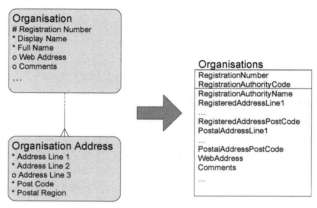

Figure 181 – De-normalising Detail Entities

As with the preceding flattened hierarchies model, we are baking in the chosen Address Types that we want to represent in our De-normalised structure.

Aggregating Detail Entity data

There is also another kind of De-normalisation to be considered in the realm of Detail Entities, and that is the aggregation of numeric Quantity and Amount data. A simplified representation of the technique is illustrated by the Order and Order Item model fragment as in figure 182.

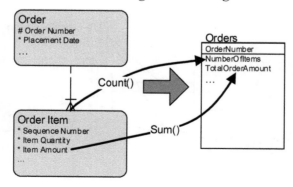

Figure 182 – De-normalising Quantities and Amounts

A: Data Modelling Approach Template

In chapter 16 it was suggested that to aid your data modelling activities you should document a Data Modelling Approach.

The following template can be used to assist you.

Title

It makes sense to give your *modelling effort* a formal Title that will help convey to other stakeholders exactly what the activity focusses on. Even if this work is being carried out to define a part of the Enterprise Logical Data Model, it is still useful to make the Title focus on the current tranche of work.

A couple of examples are:

- Client Interaction Workflow Definition
- Digital Marketing Management Augmentation

Background

Try to write a few paragraphs to briefly explain how the organisation got to the point of initiating this data modelling initiative. Try to make this as Business focussed as possible, even though it may have been triggered by the IT Function in the organisation.

Data Modelling Purpose

What are the intended outcomes and deliverables from the data modelling effort? 'Updating the Enterprise Logical Data Model' may be true, but it should not be given as the purpose of the effort.

This is because it ignores the consumer of the data model.

In fact, there are probably almost as many purposes for the work as there are key stakeholder areas. Therefore, each purpose should be consumer-centric.

You might want to use a simple table for this with Consumer and Purpose as below.

Consumer	Purpose
Enterprise Architecture	Provide an Enterprise definition required for the exchange of operational data across the organisation.
Project Manager	Define the scope of the development effort required for the Product Operational Interface Upgrade project.
Development Team	Define the definitions for the: Entities, Attributes, Domains and Mappings of the Product Operational Interface.

What you record here will be useful to help formulate your whole communication strategy and will assist you when engaging with the data model consumers. Making each purpose consumer-centric will help you frame any communications to be better targeted for their audience.

Key Stakeholders

You *must* create and maintain this list!

This is your guide as to who to include in sessions and on any communications such as emails.

It will also make you focus on the stakeholders' key contributions to your effort, for example, highlighting those who can provide input and those who will consume the output from the data modelling exercise.

Name	Title/ Role	Functional Area	Input SME	Team Member	Consumers	Key Influencer

Scope

This is one of the most difficult areas to document and you may only have a hazy notion of the Scope until you actually get started. Some of this uncertainty will depend on whether you are creating data models from scratch, or working on those that were created earlier, possibly by someone else.

Use the Conceptual Model to assist you to define the scope. It can do this because it provides the big picture and should therefore define the coarse-grained Scope.

Scoping High Level model

Sometimes a high-level visual data model of the scope can be created and stored in this document. If relevant you could make use of the Conceptual Data Model - if it exists!

However, this need not come from a formal modelling tool. Even a photo of a sketch on a whiteboard would give enough information to act as the starting point.

Part of the considerations for the scoping will be to judge how available the data is using the 'Known' and 'Knowable' challenges described in chapter 17.

In Scope

List all the Subject Areas and/or Conceptual Entities that are definitely in scope.

Also, list here any which you are not totally sure whether they are in scope or not. This is because we tend to focus continually on the items that are in scope and only occasionally the items that are out of scope. So if you put them into the Out of Scope list you will not challenge yourself to resolve them until possibly too late!

Out of Scope

List all the Subject Areas and/or Conceptual Entities that are definitely out of scope.

Timeline

There may be a Product Owner, for example that you need to work with in order to plan the activities especially if the model is immediately destined to be part of a delivery.

However, even if there is no formal Work-stream or Programme with which you are engaged, it is beneficial to create the expected timeline even if this is only a simple sketch.

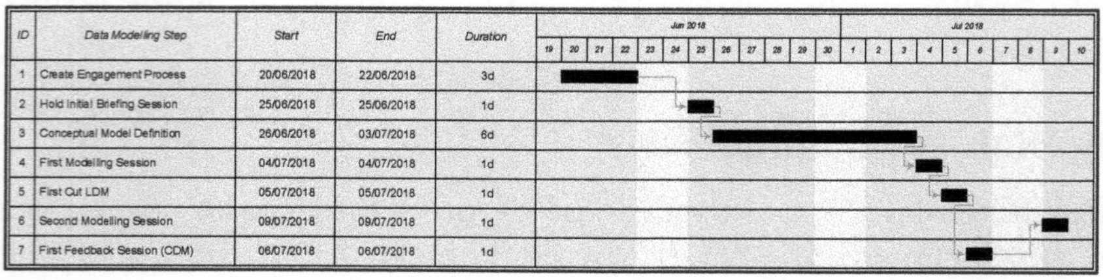

Figure 183 – A Simple data modelling timeline

You may start by planning the stages of each Subject Area at a very high level. Within each of these you can use the Standard Engagement Questions to help form the basis of your plan.

Constraints

Start to list out any constraints to the whole process such as 'Key Input SME leaving on 17th June until December.'

By recording these you will find that the planning exercise becomes easier and less prone to 'hiccups'!

B: Defining a Data Lexicon

Almost everywhere I have developed visual data models, I have used the Data Lexicon to represent the Logical Data Model in a way that is almost universally accessible.

One of the benefits of a Data Lexicon is that you are not constrained by a data modelling tool's interface and can structure your documentation in any way that helps your stakeholders to understand the definitions. So, for example, this can include text, diagrams, video and links to Internet, or Intranet items.

Here is a template that could be used as the basis for your own Lexicon with an explanation of each element.

Name	The name of the Entity.			
Synonyms	Alternative names by which the Entity is known.			
Description	A description of the Entity.			
Examples	A list of concrete examples that help to illustrate what the Entity means.			

Master Entities

Entity	Relationship description	Mandatory?	Identifying?
The Master Entity name.	A description of the Relationship.	Whether the Relationship is Mandatory at this end?	Is the Relationship an Identifying Relationship?

Keynote Attributes

Attribute Name	Type	Mandatory?	Description	Unique Identifier Number
Name of the Attribute.	The Datatype for the Attribute, for example: • Character • Number • Date • Boolean • Raw	Whether the Attribute must be recorded when the Entity instance is created.	A description of the data the Attribute holds.	This records if the Attribute is part of the Unique Identifier (0) or part of an Alternate Key (1, 2, 3, …).

Lifecycle detail	Phase	This section records the parts of the Lifecycle	Create	Details about when the Entity is created.
			Update	Details about when the Entity is updated.
			Remove	Details about when the Entity is removed.
	Description	Description of the changes in the Entity during this part of its Lifecycle		
	Rules	The Rules that may constrain the changes within the Phase		
	Privileges	The Privileges that may constrain the changes within the Phase		
Data Governance		How this Entity's data is controlled through any Data Governance processes such as Data Quality or formal Data Governance Framework?		
Data Privacy		Are there any Data Privacy constraints to how the data is stored and/or transmitted and published		
Data Retention		What are the Data Retention rules for this Entity?		
Volumes		Initial	The expected volumes for this Entity at the system go-live.	
		Final	The final or stable volumes for this Entity	
Unresolved Questions		Are there any outstanding questions about this definition including scope issues?		

You may want to simplify this template to a level you feel is appropriate. Sometimes I use a Glossary of Terms style to provide a very simple, accessible format.

Domains Of Values

The data lexicon can be used to define Domain values that have been ratified through ratification processes. Defining these inside the data model repository gives two problems:

1. Inaccessibility – these values need to be accessible across the organisation

2. Synchronisation – how will these values be maintained especially in the absence of processes to drive their maintenance

Ideally, these should be held in a specific repository for the purpose of their definition, ratification and dissemination. If this is the case, then they can be referenced in the Lexicon though Hyperlinks, for example. If there is no formal repository for this purpose, then it may be that you use something as basic as a version controlled environment, and again contain links to it from your Lexicon.

C: Implementing Super-types

In chapter 11 we discovered the technique of creating Super-types to represent Entities that exist as different manifestations in the Real World, but are treated by our organisations in very similar ways.

The different Real World manifestations form the Sub-types in our models and the common data understanding forms the Super-type Entity.

Because People and Organisations are key players in the creation and modification of the transactional data, much of it needs to be related to them. This means that they provide a good example of Sub-types and therefore can help us to illustrate potential design patterns that can be used to represent them in physical implementations.

A good technique at design stage is to provide an Interface Layer to insulate any consumers from the underlying structures as illustrated in figure 184.

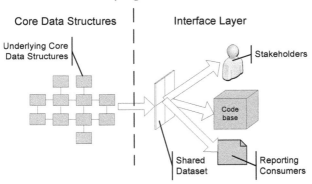

Figure 184 – An Interface Layer

This layer can be constructed using many implementation techniques, but Relational Databases can typically use either Views or Materialized Views.

Super-type Physical Resolution

There are three typical patterns to Super-type resolution which are to represent their data using:

A. A single Table

B. A single Core Table plus separate Sub-type Tables

C. Separate Tables

The following schematics illustrate the way that Views in an Interface Layer can be used to represent the different approaches.

Single Table approach

Figure 185 illustrates how Views can be used to represent Organisations and People as independent Datasets to consumers.

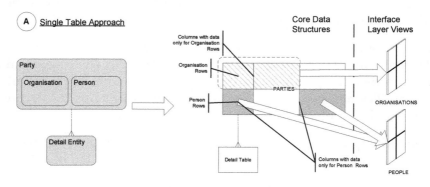

Figure 185 - Creating two Datasets from a single table

These share the same Primary Key, since this is the Primary Key from the underlying Parties Table. In this approach, any tables related to the Party table do not need to implement an Arc Foreign Key.

A benefit of this approach, is that the single Core Table is referenced by all Detail Tables using a single Foreign Key to its Primary Key.

Note that a problem arising from this approach, is that all of the underlying Columns specific to only one or other of the Sub-types, will need to be nullable. This means that in order to enforce conditional mandatory Columns for each of the Sub-types, a Check Constraint based upon the Sub-type will need to be created to enforce Not Null for those Columns. For example

type_code = 'PERSON' and

birth_date is not null

Core plus Sub-type Tables approach

In this approach, we use a single Core Table that contains the common Columns including Primary Key and create specific Sub-type Tables that contain the Columns relevant to the Sub-type. Notice that in this case, we could also use Views to create a single Parties Relation instead of, or in addition to, the separate Sub-type Views.

Figure 186 illustrates this scenario.

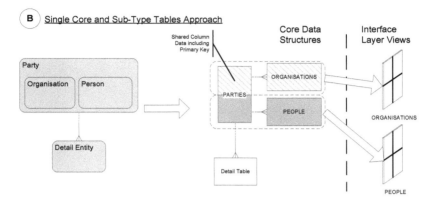

Figure 186 – Creating two Datasets from a three table approach

Any queries based purely upon the Super-type will be able to obtain their data from the single Core Table only. However, any queries that refer to Columns for the Sub-types would typically need to join between the Sub-type Tables and the Core Table. This is in addition to any other Tables they are based upon.

As illustrated in figure 186, Views can provide separate Datasets for Organisations and People, rather than all consumer queries needing to join the three Tables together.

Separate Sub-type Tables approach

In figure 187, separate Tables are created to represent Organisations and People.

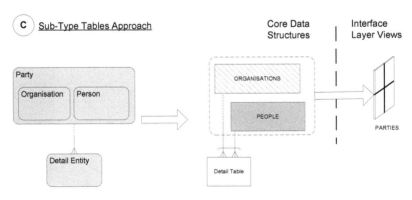

Figure 187 –Creating a consolidated Parties Dataset

However, in the Core Data Schema, to enforce Referential Integrity, the related Detail Tables will need to have *mutually exclusive Foreign Key Columns*; one referencing the Organisation Primary Key and the other, the Person Primary Key.

D: Key Point References

This Appendix provides a summary of the Key Points contained in the book.

E: Figure References

This Appendix provides a summary of the Figures contained in the book.

F: About The Author

Dave Knifton has spent nearly all of his professional life working with data, or teaching about it - and for large periods of time, doing both.

In his first few working years he was tasked to create a mathematical model of a military aircraft being developed, in order to test its flight envelope. Using the analysis outcomes from this, he worked with a team to develop the necessary flight control systems that prevented the aircraft from becoming uncontrollable and crashing! This taught him a lot about creating models of complex systems and providing feed forward and feedback data flows. The adaptive capability of the flight control systems also prefigured the current emerging discipline of Machine Learning.

The repeated theme of education first surfaced when he re-trained to become a teacher in the UK State School system. After a number of years teaching in secondary schools, he joined the newly formed Oracle UK where he became a Principal Lecturer for them.

In those early days at Oracle UK, he was fortunate to learn the basics of data modelling from Richard Barker. This experience fundamentally transformed his understanding of the significance of data. He started to appreciate databases simply as data repositories, and that actually it is the meaning of an organisation's data that is paramount. This understanding has helped to shape many dozens of solutions across the globe for the many organisations that he has provided consultancy for.

After a few years at Oracle UK, he was invited to set up Oracle Australia's Education arm. After its creation, he subsequently ran it for a number of years. Eventually, leaving Oracle, he set up and managed his own Consultancies, firstly in Sydney and then later, its sister in London. Through these he also created and spun off several commercial Web ventures.

Over many years he has delivered education to many thousands of students through Oracle, its education partners and dozens of workshops organised through his own Consultancies. Primarily this education was focussed on data related topics, including; Data Modelling, Business Analysis, Relational System Design as well as Oracle's implementation technologies.

He currently works as a Consultant Enterprise Data Architect and more recently has developed course material and lectures for Universities in the UK.

A few years ago he started to author a popular series of books on Data Architecture Fundamentals and you might find that these two are useful companions to this book:

Enterprise Data Architecture - ISBN: 978-1782223269

True Agility From Agile+DevOps - ISBN: 978-1782225225

There is also further material available on **thedatapoint.net** that you might also find useful.